PHILIP'S

C000264672

STREET ATLAS

Plymouth

First published 2007 by

Philip's, a division of
Octopus Publishing Group Ltd
2–4 Heron Quays
London E14 4JP

First edition 2007
First impression 2007

ISBN-10 0-540-09071-9
ISBN-13 978-0-540-09071-6

Photographic acknowledgements:
VI and VII James Hughes

Printed by Toppan, China

Contents

Key to map symbols

Roads

Motorway with junction number

Primary route – dual, single carriageway

A road – dual, single carriageway

B road – dual, single carriageway

Through-route – dual, single carriageway

Minor road – dual, single carriageway

Rural track, private road or narrow road in urban area

Path, bridleway, byway open to all traffic, road used as a public path

Road under construction

Pedestrianised area

Gate or obstruction to traffic restrictions may not apply at all times or to all vehicles

Parking, Park and Ride

Railways

Railway

Miniature railway

Metro station, private railway station

Emergency services

Ambulance station, coastguard station

Fire station, police station

Hospital, Accident and Emergency entrance to hospital

General features

Place of worship, Post Office

Information centre (open all year)

Bus or coach station, shopping centre

Important buildings, schools, colleges, universities and hospitals

Woods, built-up area

Tumulus FORT Non-Roman antiquity, Roman antiquity

Leisure facilities

Camping site, caravan site

Golf course, picnic site

Boundaries

Postcode boundaries

County and unitary authority boundaries

Water features

River Ouse — Tidal water, water name

Non-tidal water – lake, river, canal or stream

Lock, weir

Enlarged mapping only

Railway or bus station building

Place of interest

Parkland

Scales

Blue pages: 4½ inches to 1 mile 1:14 080

0 — 220 yds — ¼ mile — 660 yds — ½ mile

0 — 125m — 250m — 375m — ½ km

Red pages: 7 inches to 1 mile 1: 9051

0 — 110 yds — 220 yds — 330 yds — ¼ mile

0 — 125m — 250m — 375m — ½ km

Adjoining page indicators The colour of the arrow and the band indicates the scale of the adjoining page (see above)

Abbreviations

Acad	Academy	Mkt	Market
Allot Gdns	Allotments	Meml	Memorial
Cemy	Cemetery	Mon	Monument
C Ctr	Civic Centre	Mus	Museum
CH	Club House	Obsy	Observatory
Coll	College	Pal	Royal Palace
Crem	Crematorium	PH	Public House
Ent	Enterprise	Recn Gd	Recreation Ground
Ex H	Exhibition Hall	Resr	Reservoir
Ind Est	Industrial Estate	Ret Pk	Retail Park
IRB Sta	Inshore Rescue Boat Station	Sch	School
		Sh Ctr	Shopping Centre
Inst	Institute	TH	Town Hall/House
Ct	Law Court	Trad Est	Trading Estate
L Ctr	Leisure Centre	Univ	University
LC	Level Crossing	Wks	Works
Liby	Library	YH	Youth Hostel

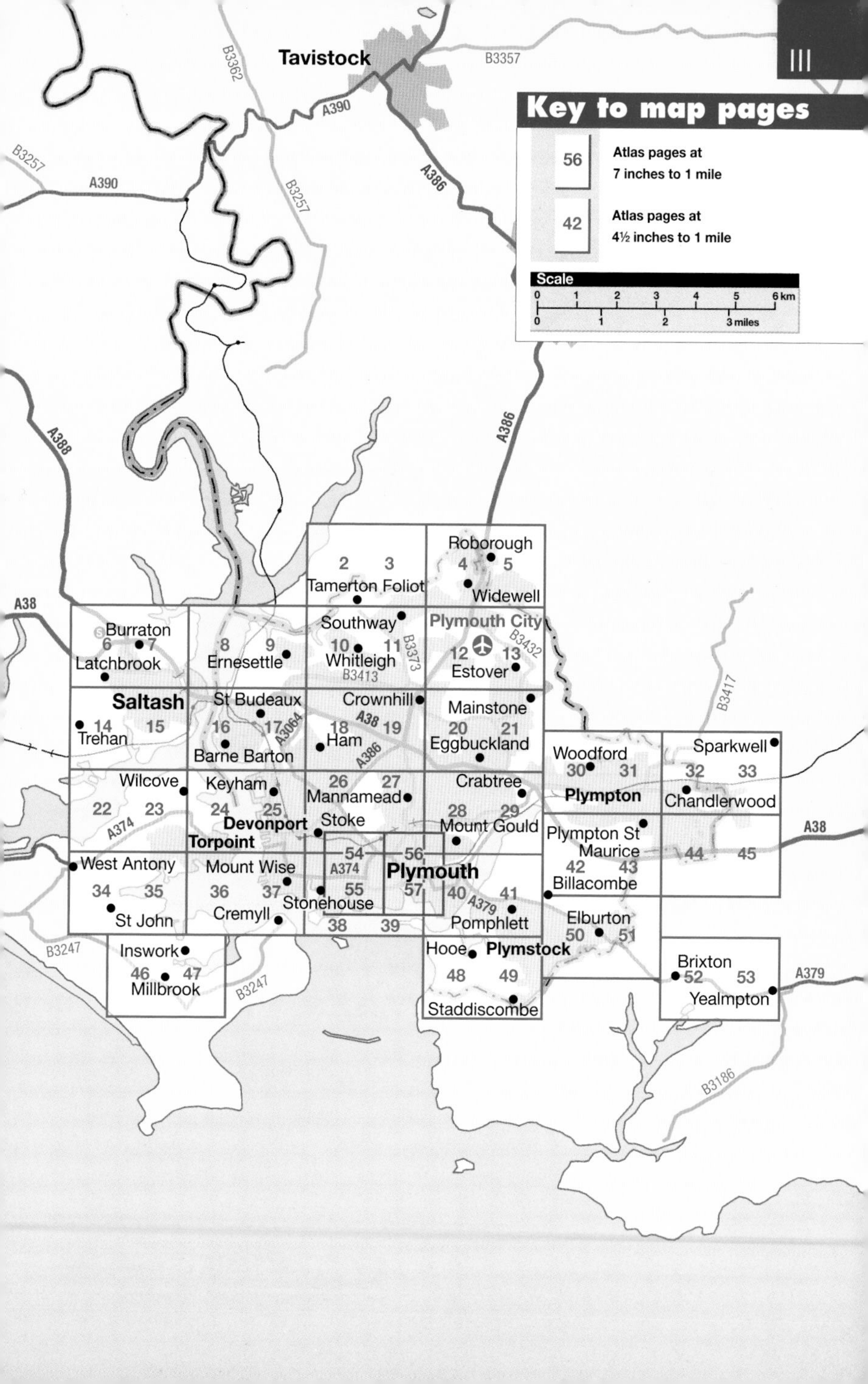
Key to map pages
56
Atlas pages at
7 inches to 1 mile
42
Atlas pages at
4½ inches to 1 mile
Scale
0 1 2 3 4 5 6 km
0 1 2 3 miles
Tavistock
B3362
B3357
A390
B3257
A390
B3257
A386
A388
A386
A38
Roborough
2 3
4 5
Tamerton Foliot
Widewell
Burraton
6 7
Latchbrook
8 9
Ernesettle
Southway
10 11
Whitleigh
B3413
B3373
Plymouth City
12 13
Estover
B3432
Saltash
14 15
Trehan
St Budeaux
16 17
Barne Barton
A3064
Crownhill
A38
18 19
Ham
A386
Mainstone
20 21
Eggbuckland
Woodford
30 31
Plympton
Sparkwell
32 33
Chandlerwood
B3417
Wilcove
22 23
A374
Keyham
24 25
Devonport
Torpoint
26 27
Mannamead
Stoke
Crabtree
28 29
Mount Gould
Plympton St Maurice
42 43
Billacombe
44 45
A38
West Antony
34 35
St John
Mount Wise
36 37
Cremyll
Stonehouse
54
A374
55
56
Plymouth
57
38 39
40 41
A379
Pomphlett
Elburton
50 51
Hooe
Plymstock
48 49
Staddiscombe
Brixton
52 53
Yealmpton
A379
B3247
Inswork
46 47
Millbrook
B3247
B3186

Mushton
Polborder
Tremoan
Mt. Ararat
Quay
Hole's Hole
Leeches
Collytown
Weir Quay
Pentillie Castle
Rowse
Clamoak
Ley
Maristow
Gnatham
Mt. Jessop
Paynter's Cross
Crosspark Wood
RIVER TAMAR
Pillaton
Kernock
Stockadon
Tinnell
New Park
Sillaton
Haye
BERE FERRERS
Bere Ferrers
Pillatonmill
Smeaton
Ellbridge
Wayton
Thorn Pt.
RIVER TAVY
Blaxton
Coombe
Cargreen
West Kingsmill
Villaton
Cuttivett
Hatt Ho.
Landulph Cross
River Lynher
Weir Pt.
Warleigh Ho.
Hatt
Botusfleming
Landulph
Tavy Bri.
Wotton Cross
Moditonham Quay
Neal Pt.
Kingsmill Lake
Warleigh Pt.
Tamerton Foliot
Notter
Skinham Pt.
Warren Pt.
Lantallock Cross
Notter Bri.
Carkeel
Landrake
SALTASH SERVICES
Whitleigh
Whity Cross
PLYMOUT
B3271
South Pill
Trewint
Trematon
Ernesettle
Burraton
B3413
St. Erney
Treluggan Manor
Tamar Br.
Toll
SALTASH
Honicknowle
Markwell
Burraton Coombe
Wearde
SALTASH
St. Stephen's
St. Budeaux
Port Eliot
Burell
Forder
Riverside
King's Tamerton
Trevollard
Trehan
MARY NEWMAN'S COTTAGE
VICTORIA RD.
FERRY RD.
A38
St. Germans
Trematon Castle
Weston Mill
Pennycross
Elm Gate
Wearde Quay
Barne Barton
Ham
Grove
Antony Passage
St. Germans Quay
Shillingham
TAMAR VALLEY
ANTONY HOUSE (N.T.)
Wilcove
KEYHAM
A3064
A386
A374
St. Germans or Lynher River
Jupiter Pt.
P&R
Pevere
Ince Castle
Hamoaze
Dockyard
Devonport
HOME PARK
Erth
Antony Ho.
Ford
Central Park
Erth Hill
A374
DOCKYARD
B3396
Horsoh Fm.
Maryfield
Stoke
DEVONPORT
PLYMOUTH
Haye
Berry Down
Torpoint
Sheviock
H.M.S. Fisgard
MERCHANT'S HOUSE
A374
B3247
Antony
H.M.S. Raleigh
A374
Trethill
Crafthole
Deadman's Pt.
Wolsdon Ho.
St. John's Lake
Stonehouse
Blerrick
B3247
Sango I.
Mount Wise
The Hoe
Lr. Tregantle
St. John
Cremyll
PLYMOUTH
Trethill Cliffs
Penhale
Devil's Pt.
Mount
Long Sands
B3247
Empacombe
Barn Pool
Southdown
Inswork
Drake's Island
Tregantle Cliff
Millbrook Lake
MOUNT EDGCUMBE
Sharrow Pt.
Millbrook
The Bridge
Withnoe
Freathy
B3247
Anderton
The Sound
Maker Heights
Picklecombe Pt
Trenninow
Tregonhawke
Wiggle
Cawsand Bay
Breakwater
SOUTH WEST COAST PATH
Kingsand
Forder
Cawsand
Pier Cellars
Polhawn Cove
Rame
ROSCOFF 6:00
SANTANDER 18:00
(MAR-NOV)
Queener Pt.
Penlee Pt.
Chapel
Rame Head
Route planning
Scale
0
1
2
3
4 km

V
492
Bickham
Hen Tor
River Plym
Wigford Down
Goodameavy
Cadover Bri.
Trowlesworthy Warren
Lee Moor
Trowlesworthy Tors 348
Lr. Upperton
North Wood
West Down
Shell Top 475
Penn Moor
Shaugh Prior
Shaugh Moor
Blackaton Cross
Roborough Ho.
Leigh
Nethershaugh Fm.
Lee Moor Ho.
Hawks Tor
Penn Beacon 427
Beatland Corner
Roborough
Bickleigh
Bickleigh Down
Bickleigh Vale
Wotter
Lee Moor
Tolchmoor Gate
Rook Tor
Widewell
Woolwell
Clay Works
Newpark Waste
Hele Cross
P&R
Glenholt
Gt. Shaugh Wood
Reservoir
Rook
Piall Bri.
CITY
Plym Forest
Brixton Barton
Portworthy
Crownhill Down
Heddon Down
Derriford
Boringdon Camp
Industrial Estate
Cann Wood
Lutton
Cornwood
A386
Fursdon
B3432
Bude Fm.
Drakeland Corner
DARTMOOR WILDLIFE PARK
Yondertown
Moor Cross
Crownhill
Estover
Mainstone
Plym Bri.
Tory Bt.
B3417
Bottle Hill
Slade
B3413
Leigham
Newnham Park
Hemerdon Ball 212
Eggbuckland
Boringdon
PLYM VALLEY RLY.
Old Newnham
Hemerdon
Sparkwell
Beechwood
Gt. Stert
THE PARKWAY
Longbridge
STA.
Woodford
Farde
Compton
R. Yealm
Efford
Crabtree
Plympton
B3416
Chaddlewood
Venton
Langage
Castle (rems. of)
Lee Mill
Industrial Estate
Laira
A374
Underwood
SALTRAM HOUSE (N.T.)
Plympton St. Maurice
Voss
A38
Smithaleigh
Mount Gould
River Plym
Strashle
Haye Fm.
Southwood Wood
Chookford
Wiverton
Brook
People's Bri.
A379
Billacombe
E. Sherford
Coyton
Cattedown
Pomphlett
Hareston Fm.
Lotherton Bri.
Oreston
W. Sherford
Lyneham Ho.
Cattewater
Worston
Plymstock
Elburton
Gorlofen
Wollaton
Stonycross
Wilburton
Long B
Chittleburn
Yeo Park
Halwell
Hooe
Goosewell
Brixton
Way Fm.
Yealmpton
Combe
Yealmbridge
Dunstone
Spriddlestone
Winston
Kitley
Kitley Cave
Torr
Staddiscombe
Spriddlestone Ho.
Ramsland
Hollacombe Hill
Crebar
Raneleigh
Warren Pt.
Ford
Wembury Wood
Cofflete Creek
Wrescombe
Down Thomas
R. Yealm
Luson
Knighton
Gnaton Hall
Manor Bourne
Collaton Fm.
Creacombe Fm.
West Wembury
RAF Station
B3186
Borough Fm.
Bay
Wembury Ho.
Butts Park
HMS Cambridge
Wembury
Newton Ferrers
Pamfl
New Barton
Pool Mill Fm.
Alston Hall
Battisborough Cross
Wembury Pt.
Blackstone Rocks
Membland
Season Pt.
Warren Pt.
Bridgend
Wembury Bay
Carswell
Mothecombe
Mouthstone Pt.
Noss Mayo
Lambside
St. Anchorite's Rock
Mew Stone
Worswell
Rowden Fm.
Bugle Hole
Erme Mouth
Gara Pt.
The Warren
Beacon Hill
Blackattery Pt.
Butcher's Cove
Stoke Ho.
Ivy I.
Battisborough I.
Cunnimall
Blackstone Pt.
Netton Fm.
Fernycomb Beach

Sights of Plymouth

Museums and Galleries

Elizabethan House★ *New Street* Genuine Tudor sea captain's home with period furniture, fabrics, sloping oak floors, and Elizabethan kitchen and garden. ☎01752 304774 www.plymouth.gov.uk 57 A2

The Green House *The Ride, Chelson Meadow* An interactive environment centre. Arcade style games with an educational twist. www.thegreenhouseplymouth.org.uk ☎01752 665024 41 C3

Merchant's House★ *St Andrew Street* Fine 16th century residence. Victorian artefacts, curiosities, documents and photographs. Schoolroom and chemist's shop. ☎01752 304775 www.plymouth.gov.uk 55 C2

Plymouth Arts Centre *Looe Street* Exhibitions by local, national and international artists. Hosts independent and foreign films. Restaurant. www.plymouthac.org.uk ☎01752 206114 56 A2

Plymouth City Museum & Art Gallery★ *Drake Circus* Displays of natural history, art and maritime. Regular talks, concerts and workshops. Permanent and temporary exhibitions. www.plymouth.gov.uk ☎01752 304775 56 A3

Historic Sites

Crownhill Fort *Crownhill Fort Road* A Royal Commission fort built in 1872. Beautifully restored by the Landmark Trust. ☎01752 793754 www.crownhillfort.co.uk 11 C1

Fort Bovisand *Bovisand* Built to defend Plymouth Sound, it is next to Bovisand Harbour and now used as a diving centre. Explore the underground drying rooms. www.plymouth.gov.uk 48 A1

Mayflower Steps *Barbican* The site from where the Pilgrim Fathers departed when setting out to cross the Atlantic Ocean. www.mayflowersteps.co.uk 57 A1

Prysten House *Finewell Street* A 15th century house with well and courtyard. The oldest domestic dwelling in Plymouth. Linked to St Andrew's church. ☎01752 661414 55 C2

Royal Citadel★ *Hoe Road, Barbican* Completed in 1666 with 70 foot walls it was Plymouth's most important defence in its early years. Guided tours available. Fisher's Nose Blockhouse is on the south east corner, dating from 1490. ☎01476 871000 www.english-heritage.org.uk 55 C1

Places of Worship

St Andrew's Church *Royal Parade* Early recordings of a church on this site from 8th century. Heavily bombed in the Second World War. www.standrewschurch.org.uk ☎01752 661414 55 C2

St Mary and St Boniface RC Cathedral *Cecil Street* Built in 1858, designed by Charles and Joseph Hanson. ☎01752 662537 www.plymouthcathedral.org.uk 54 B3

Other Sights

Antony House *Torpoint* Early 18th century house with extensive grounds and gardens. Great number of paintings, furniture and tapestries. www.nationaltrust.org.uk ☎01752 812191 22 A3

The Barbican★★ *Adjacent to Sutton Harbour* A maze of narrow streets with many art galleries and unique shops. Also a working harbour, take trips around the Naval Dockyards. www.plymouthbarbican.com ☎01822 853607 57 A2

Barbican Glass Works *The Old Fishmarket, Barbican* Transformed from the old fishmarket, watch the traditional skills of the glassblowers. Main stockist of Dartington Crystal with giftshop. ☎01752 224777 www.plymouthbarbican.com 57 A2

Buckland Abbey★ *Yelverton* Home of Sir Francis Drake, this 700 year old house has a fine 16th century great hall, and is famously haunted. www.nationaltrust.org.uk ☎01822 853607

Mary Newman's Cottage *Culver Road, Saltash* Thought to be the home of Sir Francis Drake's first wife. Built in 15th century with cottage garden. Contemporary furniture loaned by the Victoria and Albert Museum. www.enjoyengland.com ☎01752 262072 16 A4

Mayflower International Marina *Ocean Quay, Richmond Walk* Independent marina with fantastic facilities. ☎01752 556633 www.mayflowermarina.co.uk 37 C2

Mount Edgcumbe *Cremyll, Torpoint* Restored Tudor mansion house with French, Italian and English formal gardens. 800 acres of parkland. www.enjoyengland.com ☎01752 822236 37 B1

Naval History Library *Central Library, Drake Circus* Resources to study naval history. Items cover the Royal Navy, Nato and European and Commonwealth navies. www.plymouth.gov.uk ☎01752 305909 56 A3

Plym Valley Railway *Marsh Mills Station, Coypool Road, Plympton* Recreation of ex-Great Western line in the 1950 and 1960's period. Preserved steam and diesel locomotives. ☎01752 305909 www.plymrail.co.uk 30 A3

Plymouth Gin *Southside Street, Barbican* Tour the 15th century Black Friars Distillery showing the history of gin. Distillery shop and exclusive private tasting master classes. ☎01752 665292 www.plymouthgin.com 57 A2

Saltram House *Plympton* Magnificent Georgian mansion with original furniture and paintings. Landscaped park overlooks Plym estuary. ☎0115 950 0411 www.nationaltrust.org.uk 42 A4

Smeaton's Tower *The Hoe* A lighthouse with panoramic views over the city and beyond. Originally on the Eddystone Rocks, it was moved stone by stone in the 1880s. ☎01752 603300 www.visitplymouth.info 55 C1

▼ *Plymouth Hoe*

Green Spaces

Central Park *Alma Road* Large park to the north of Plymouth. Picnic areas. Adult size keep-fit trail with apparatus around the park. Childrens play parks. Sports complex with swimming and diving pool. www.plymouth.gov.uk 26 C2
Dartmoor National Park★★ Some 368 square miles of moorland, deep wooded gorges and rocky rivers, interspersed with thriving market towns and villages. www.dartmoor-npa.gov.uk
Devonport Park *Paradise Road, Devonport* Park with playground, tennis courts, sports pitches, bowling green, pavilion, floral displays and panoramic views of Devonport Dockyard. www.plymouth.gov.uk 25 C1
The Garden House★ *Buckland Monachorum, Yelverton* Enchanting 8 acre garden around 16th century ruins. Georgian tearoom and plant sales centre. 01822 854769 www.thegardenhouse.org.uk
Mount Wise Park *Richmond Walk, Mount Wise* Panoramic views over Mount Edgecumbe and Drakes Island, playground, nature areas and The Scott Memorial. www.plymouth.gov.uk 37 C3
Plym Bridge Woods *Access from Estover or Plympton via Plymbridge Lane* Part of the Lower Plym Valley, some 200 acres of woodland. Family walks, bird watching and cycle rides, as well as a good education site. www.nationaltrust.org 21 C4
Plymouth Hoe★ *Adjacent to the Barbican* Large park with views over Plymouth Sound. Contains a fun park with crazy golf, trampolines and mini-marina. Also has a sensory garden. Memorials to RAF, Naval War, Armada and Drake Statue. 55 C2

Activities

Barbican Leisure Park *Barbican Approach, Coxside* Multiplex cinema, 10-pin bowling, restaurants, bars, nightclubs and health and fitness suite. www.plymouth.gov.uk 56 C1
Barbican Theatre *Castle Street* Previously the Serenade Arts building, it has undergone radical refurbishment. Holds drama and dance performances and writing classes. www.barbicantheatre.co.uk 01752 222209 57 A1
Brickfields Sports Centre *Madden Road, Devonport* Full size floodlit all weather pitch, athletics track, senior and junior grass football pitches and grass rugby pitch. 0870 300 0040 www.plymouth.gov.uk 37 C4
Drake Circus *Charles Street* New shopping centre with late night openings. 45 high street shops, restaurants, cafés and over 1200 parking spaces. 01752 223030 www.drakecircus.com 56 A3
Mount Batten Centre *Lawrence Road, Mount Batten* RYA dinghy sailing, power boating and wind surfing, in a relaxed and clean environment. www.mount-batten-centre.com 01752 404567 39 C1

▼ *National Marine Aquarium*

National Marine Aquarium★★ *Rope Walk, Coxside* Britain's biggest and deepest aquarium, focusing on education and conservation. Explore the underwater tunnel with over 3000 fish on display from sharks to seahorses. Lots of interactive and hands-on attractions. 01752 600301 www.national-aquarium.co.uk 57 A2
Plymouth Argyle FC *Home Park* Founded in 1886, this is the home ground for the Plymouth Pilgrims. 01752 822236 www.pafc.premiumtv.co.uk 26 C3
Plymouth Athenaeum & Theatre *Derrys Cross* First started in 1812, today it is a Cultural Society. The theatre holds performances by amateur and professional companies. www.plymouthathenaeum.co.uk 01752 266104 55 B2
Plymouth Beer Festival In association with CAMRA, up to 200 real ales available. Various festivals annually throughout Plymouth. www.plymouthcamra.co.uk
Plymouth Farmers Market *Pannier Market, Cornwall Street* 25 stalls with products reared, grown and made by local farmers. 01752 306551 www.plymouth.gov.uk 54 B3
Plymouth Folk Roots An annual music festival bringing music, song and dance throughout Plymouth. Seasonal concerts and many events throughout the year. 01752 564847 www.plymouthfolkfestival.com
Plymouth Maritime Services *Phoenix Wharf, Barbican* Services provided by the City Council for managing and mooring boats. Available for hire. 01752 304304 www.plymouth.gov.uk 57 A2
Plymouth Parkway *Bolitho Park, Manadon Football Development Centre* Flood lit all weather pitch for the local community. www.plymouth.gov.uk 19 A3
Plymouth Pavilions *Millbay Road* Large range of live entertainment. Concerts, sports events, ice rink and fun swimming pool. www.plymouthpavilions.com 0845 146 1460 55 B2
Plymouth Ski Centre *Alpine Park, Marsh Mills* Ski, snowboard and blading centre for all levels. Wide variety of activities and lessons available. www.plymouthskislope.co.uk 01752 600220 21 B1
Plymouth Youth Sailing Club *Plymouth Sound* Water sports club with full supervision, to help develop racing and seamanship skills. www.plymouth-youth-sailing.info 39 C1
South West Coast Path Britain's longest National Trail with two UNESCO World Heritage Sites on route. 01752 896237 www.swcp.org.uk
Theatre Royal *Royal Parade* Musicals, drama and dance. www.theatreroyal.com 01752 668282 55 C2
Waterfront Walkway A 10 mile walk following the water's edge from Admiral's Hard to Jennycliff, passing the Mayflower Steps, shops and pubs. www.plymouth.gov.uk

Information

Tourist Information
Plymouth: 3-5 The Barbican 01752 306330 57 A2
Plymouth City Council
Civic Centre, Royal Parade 01752 668000 www.plymouth.gov.uk 55 C2
Car Parking City Council
01752 304021 www.plymouth.gov.uk
Car Parking NCP
0870 606 7050 www.ncp.co.uk
National Rail Enquiries
0845 748 4950 www.nationalrail.co.uk
Local Bus and Rail
0870 608 2608 www.traveline.org.uk

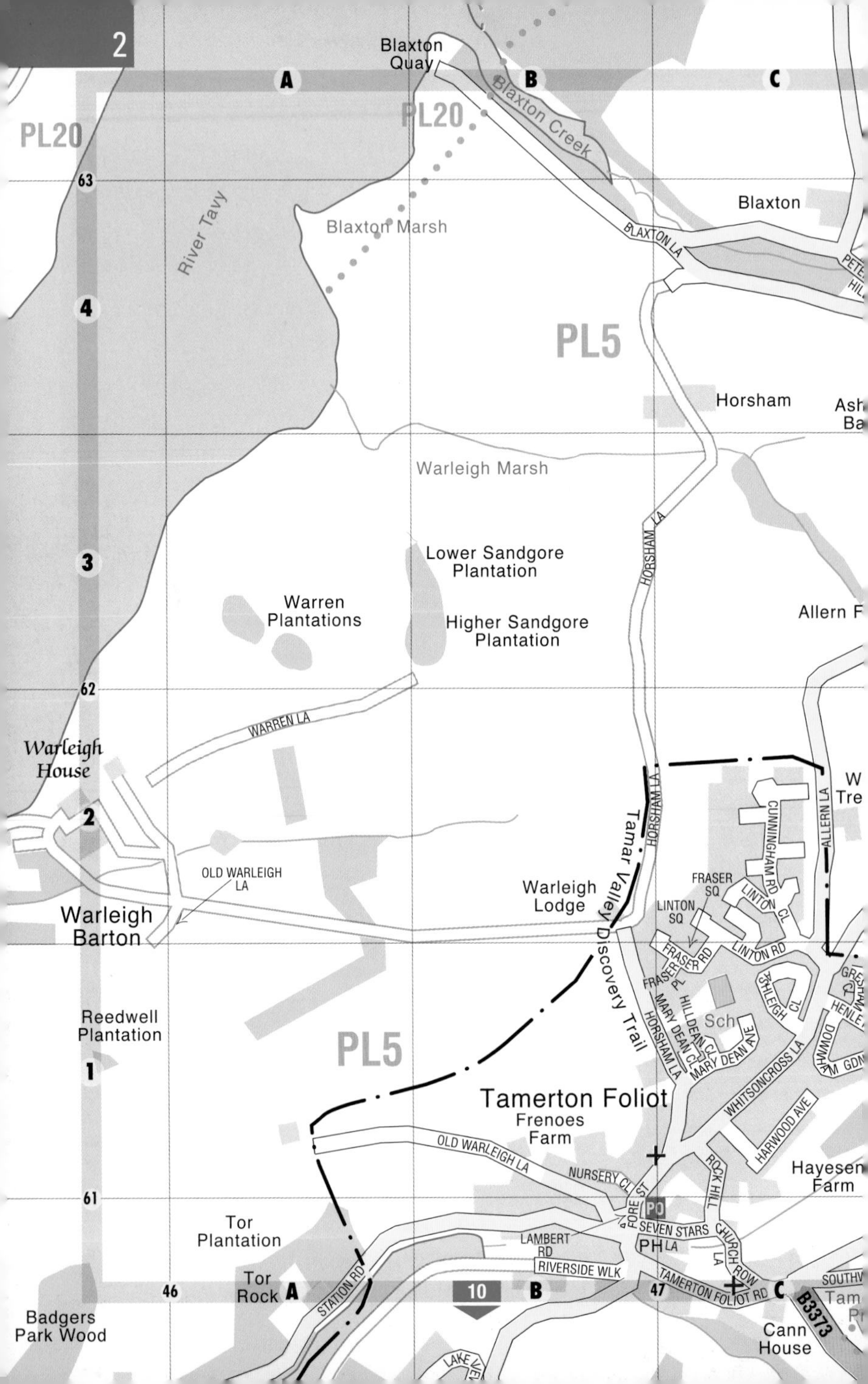
Blaxton Quay
A
B
C
PL20
PL20
Blaxton Creek
63
River Tavy
Blaxton Marsh
Blaxton
BLAXTON LA
4
PL5
Horsham
Warleigh Marsh
HORSHAM LA
Lower Sandgore Plantation
3
Warren Plantations
Higher Sandgore Plantation
Allern F
62
WARREN LA
Warleigh House
2
HORSHAM LA
ALLERN LA
CUNNINGHAM RD
Tamar Valley Discovery Trail
OLD WARLEIGH LA
Warleigh Lodge
FRASER SQ
LINTON CL
LINTON SQ
Warleigh Barton
FRASER RD
LINTON RD
FRASER PL
ASHLEIGH CL
MARY DEAN CL
HILLDEAN CL
Sch
Reedwell Plantation
HORSHAM LA
MARY DEAN AVE
PL5
1
WHITSONCROSS LA
Tamerton Foliot
Frenoes Farm
HARWOOD AVE
OLD WARLEIGH LA
Hayesend Farm
NURSERY CL
ROCK HILL
61
FORE ST
PO
Tor Plantation
LAMBERT RD
SEVEN STARS LA
PH
CHURCH LA
CHURCH ROW
RIVERSIDE WLK
Tor Rock
STATION RD
46
A
10
B
47
TAMERTON FOLIOT RD
C
B3373
Badgers Park Wood
Cann House

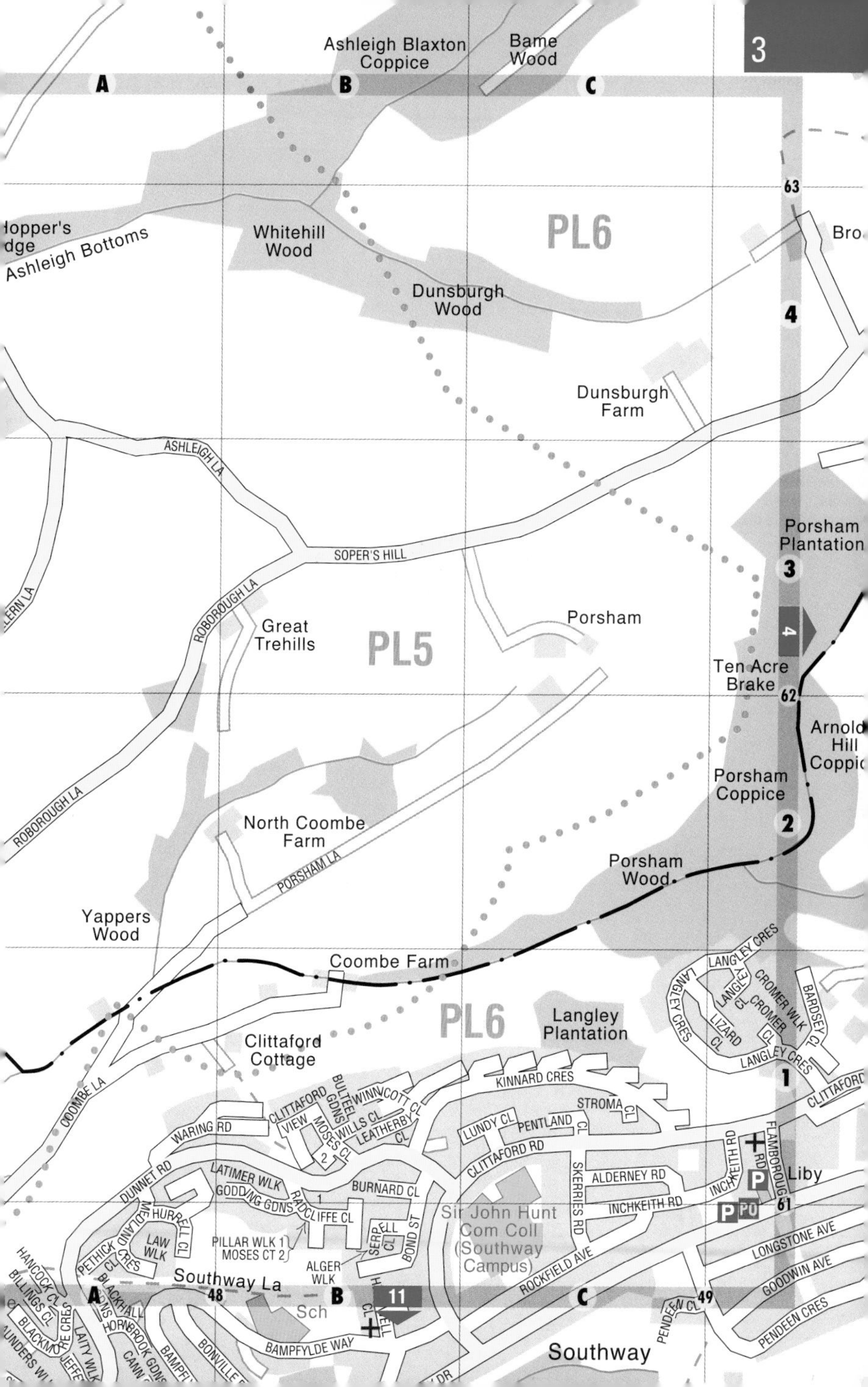
Ashleigh Blaxton Coppice
Bame Wood
A
B
C
PL6
Hopper's
Edge
Ashleigh Bottoms
Whitehill Wood
Dunsburgh Wood
Bro
63
4
Dunsburgh Farm
ASHLEIGH LA
SOPER'S HILL
ROBOROUGH LA
Porsham Plantation
3
Great Trehills
PL5
Porsham
Ten Acre Brake
62
Arnold Hill Coppice
Porsham Coppice
2
North Coombe Farm
PORSHAM LA
Porsham Wood
Yappers Wood
Coombe Farm
PL6
Langley Plantation
Clittaford Cottage
LANGLEY CRES
CROMER WLK
CROMER CL
LIZARD CL
BARDSEY CL
1
KINNARD CRES
CLITTAFORD RD
COOMBE LA
WARING RD
CLITTAFORD VIEW
BULTEEL GDNS
WINNICOTT CL
MOSES CL
WILLS CL
LEATHERBY CL
LUNDY CL
PENTLAND CL
STROMA CL
FLAMBOROUGH RD
KEITH RD
DUNNET RD
LATIMER WLK
GODDING GDNS
RADCLIFFE CL
BURNARD CL
SKERRIES RD
ALDERNEY RD
INCHKEITH RD
Liby
61
HURRELL CL
MEDLAND CRES
LAW WLK
PETHICK CL
PILLAR WLK 1
MOSES CT 2
ALGER WLK
SERPELL CL
BOND ST
Sir John Hunt Com Coll (Southway Campus)
ROCKFIELD AVE
LONGSTONE AVE
GOODWIN AVE
HANCOCK CL
BILLINGS CL
BLACKHALL
Southway La
48
11
49
PENDEEN CL
PENDEEN CRES
Sch
BLACKMORE CRES
LAITY WLK
HORNBROOK GDNS
BAMPFYLDE WAY
BONVILLE
Southway

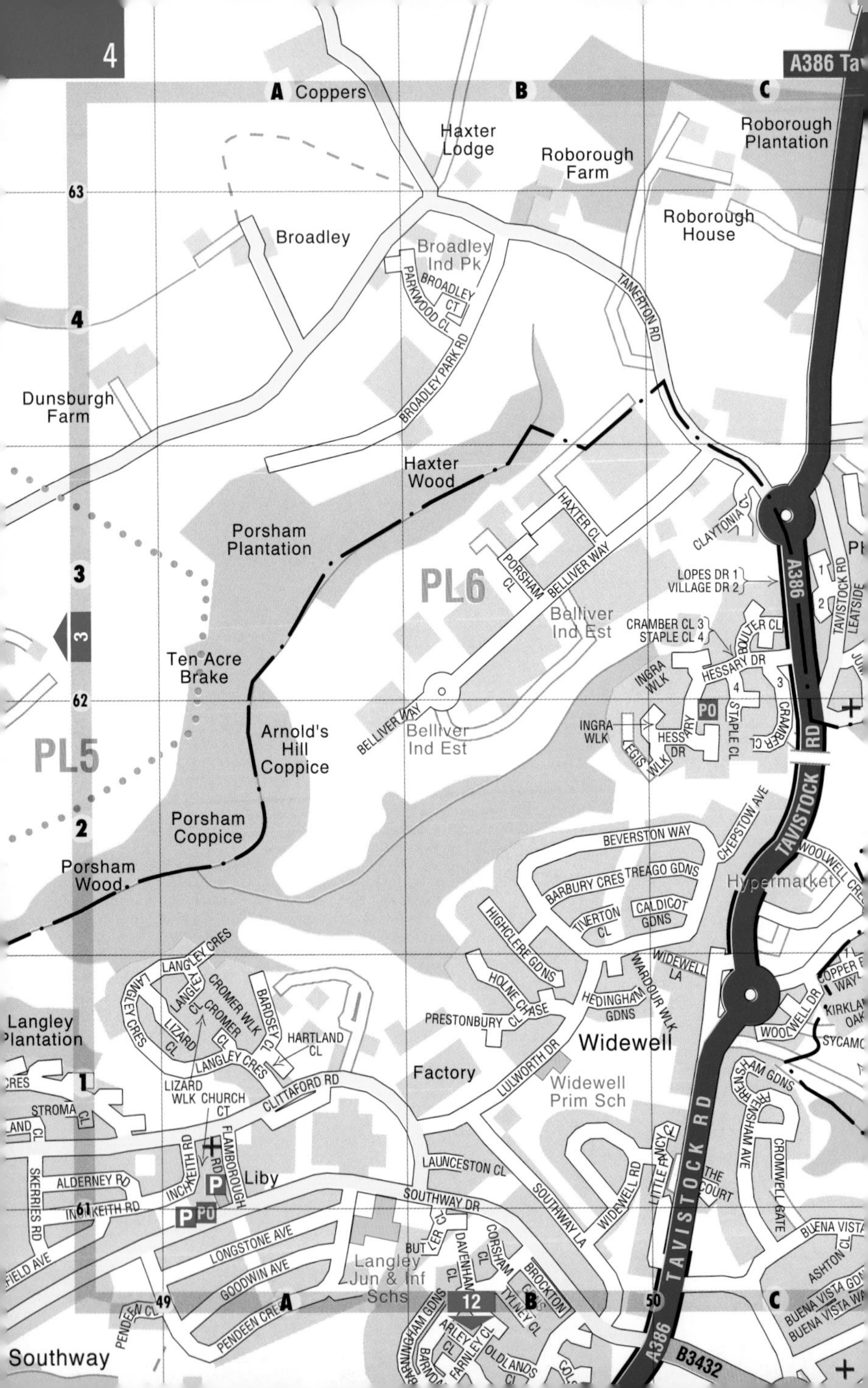

A386 Ta
A
Coppers
B
C
Haxter Lodge
Roborough Farm
Roborough Plantation
Roborough House
63
Broadley
Broadley Ind Pk
BROADLEY CT
PARKWOOD CL
TAMERTON RD
4
BROADLEY PARK RD
Dunsburgh Farm
Haxter Wood
Porsham Plantation
HAXTER CL
CLAYTONIA CL
PORSHAM CL
BELLIVER WAY
PL6
LOPES DR 1
VILLAGE DR 2
A386
3
Belliver Ind Est
CRAMBER CL 3
STAPLE CL 4
BOULTER CL
TAVISTOCK RD
LEATSIDE
Ten Acre Brake
INGRA WLK
HESSARY DR
62
BELLIVER WAY
Belliver Ind Est
PO
STAPLE CL
CRAMBER CL
Arnold's Hill Coppice
INGRA WLK
HESSARY DR
LEGIS WLK
PL5
TAVISTOCK RD
2
CHEPSTOW AVE
Porsham Coppice
BEVERSTON WAY
Porsham Wood
TREAGO GDNS
BARBURY CRES
Hypermarket
WOOLWELL CRES
TIVERTON CL
CALDICOT GDNS
HIGHCLERE GDNS
LANGLEY CRES
WIDEWELL LA
COPPER WAY
HOLNE CHASE
WARDOUR WLK
HEDINGHAM GDNS
LANGLEY CL
CROMER WLK
BARDSEY CL
Langley Plantation
LANGLEY CRES
LIZARD CL
CROMER CL
HARTLAND CL
PRESTONBURY CL
WOOLWELL DR
KIRKLAND OAK
SYCAMORE
Widewell
LANGLEY CRES
Factory
LULWORTH DR
FRENSHAM GDNS
1
CRES
LIZARD WLK
CHURCH CT
CLITTAFORD RD
Widewell Prim Sch
STROMA CL
LAND CL
FLAMBOROUGH RD
INCHKEITH RD
LITTLE FANCY CL
FRENSHAM AVE
CROMWELL GATE
SKERRIES RD
ALDERNEY RD
Liby
LAUNCESTON CL
WIDEWELL RD
TAVISTOCK RD
THE COURT
61
INCHKEITH RD
SOUTHWAY DR
SOUTHWAY LA
P
PO
BUENA VISTA
ASHTON CL
FIELD AVE
LONGSTONE AVE
BUTLER CL
DAVENHAM CL
CORSHAM CL
BROCKTON
Langley Jun & Inf Schs
GOODWIN AVE
TYLNEY CL
49
A
12
B
50
C
BUENA VISTA GDNS
BUENA VISTA WAY
PENDEEN CL
PENDEEN CRES
BARNINGHAM GDNS
ARLEY CL
FARNLEY CL
OLDLANDS CL
A386
B3432
Southway

A
B
C
LITTLE DOWN LA
Leigh
PL6
HELE LA
63
Hele
4
LEIGH LA
Vicarage
NEW RD
Barracks
HELE CL
Coombe
Barton
Roborough
BLACKEVEN HILL
3
NEW RD
HATSHILL
FARM CL
Coombe
Wood
BICKLEIGH DOWN RD
Hursley
Bsns Pk
62
Bickleigh Down
Rock
Wood
1 BLACKTHORN CL
2 BRACKEN CL
Pick Pie
Plantation
REDWING
DR
1 ROCKWOOD RD
2 CHURCH PARK CT
3 CHURCHLANDS RD
2
KESTREL CL
MERLIN CL
SKYLARK RISE
PICK PIE DR
HEDGEROW
CL
NEW WOOD
CL
DARKLAKE LA
VIOLET DR
CLOVER RISE
CHURCH PARK RD
FERNDALE CL
CAMPION
VIEW
PO
SCHOOL
DR
Sch
CHURCHLANDS
CL
BOWERS PARK DR
SPRING PK
HOLMER
DOWN
WOODEND RD
Darklake
THE HEATHERS
CANN WOOD VIEW
PL6
MEADOWLANDS
CORNER
BRAKE
ROSEHIP CL
COPPERS
PK
HONEYSUCKLE
CL
WARREN
PK
FOREST VIEW
VALLEY
VIEW
TRAMWAY RD
1
PINEWOOD DR
Woolwell
THISTLE CL
MULBERRY
CL
ROWAN WAY
BIRCH CL
TRENDLEWOOD RD 1
ASHTREE CL 2
OAKWOOD CL 3
MAPLE WAY
LARCH DR
61
West Wood
West Devon Way
Darklake
Wood
A
51
B
13
C
52
GLENHOLT CL
WOODFORD RD
Glenholt
JASMINE
GDNS
HOLTWOOD RD
VALLEY WLK

Botusfleming
PH
Moditonha House
Smallacombe
Clark's Lake
A388 Launceston
East Town Farm
Woodside Racing Stables
A388
Atuba
PINKHAMS COTTS
Carkeel
Broadmoor Wood
CARKEEL BARNS
Carkeel Farm
DIRTY LA
EDGCUMBE RD
PRIDEAUX
LIBBY CT
AVERY
Saltash Service Area
PL12
A38
A38 Liskeard
Peninsular Pk
FORGE LA
CHANNON RD
B3271
Saltash Bsns Pk
LONG RD
Moorlands Trad Est
LONG ACRE
Saltash Parkway Ind Est
WHITY CROSS
LISKEARD RD
BURRATON RD
MOORLANDS LA
NORTH PARK VILLAS
SMITHY CL
CALLINGTON
WOOD ACRE
TAYLOR RD
PH
LISKEARD RD
BARROW DOWN
SMITHS WAY
PLOUGH GN
MOTE PK
Latchbrook
BUTTERDOWN 1
SMITHFIELD DR 2
HIGHFIELD PK 3
HEARL RD
PONDFIELD RD
LEAT VIEW
CHAPEL RD
WOOD CL
CLOVER WLK
GRENFELL GDNS
PROSPECT LA
Sch
COOK CT
THORN LA
CHAPMAN CT
HOBBS CRES
GALLACHER WAY
HALLETT CL
SNELL DR
LANGERWELL CL
HERITAGE CL
RUSSELL CT
PORTER WAY
FORSYTHIA DR
LARCH CL
MEWS
FOXGLOVE WAY 4
THE HEDGEROWS 5
MIDDLEFIELD CL
SYCAMORE
FAIRMEAD
THE CLOSE
RUSSELL CL
OAK
CARRISBROOKE WAY
YELLOW TOR RD
ASHBURGH PARC
RD
THE KEEP
FAIRMEAD RD
MILCH PK
THE COURT
BEWEYS PK
Latchbrook Leat
EDWARDS CRES
THE SPEARES
SPIRE HILL PK
6 LANGERWE
7 PROSPECT
8 THE GREEN
9 ELM COTTS
10 THE SQUA
11 SOUTHFIE
Wadgeworthy Farm
A
B
C
40
41
61
60
59
4
3
2
1
14
LINNET CT
ROWAN CT
TWO HILLS
HAWKS PK
TINC
WENTWORTH
Burraton

Moditonham Quay
The Marsh
South Down
Kingsmill Lake
Burrhills Farm
Burrhills Quay
Skinham Point
Skinham Creek
Hole Wood
Chine Fleet Country Club
Quarryfield Coppice
Tamar View Ind Est
PL12
Tamar Park
Saltash Ind Est
Pill Farm
PILL LA
Mill Park
BEAUMONT TERR
Saltmill Creek
Burraton
A38
B3271
NEW RD
NORTH RD
South Pill
Saltash Leisure Ctr
Liby
Brunel Prim Sch
Cornwall Coll Saltash
St Barnabas
Saltash
61
60
59
42
43

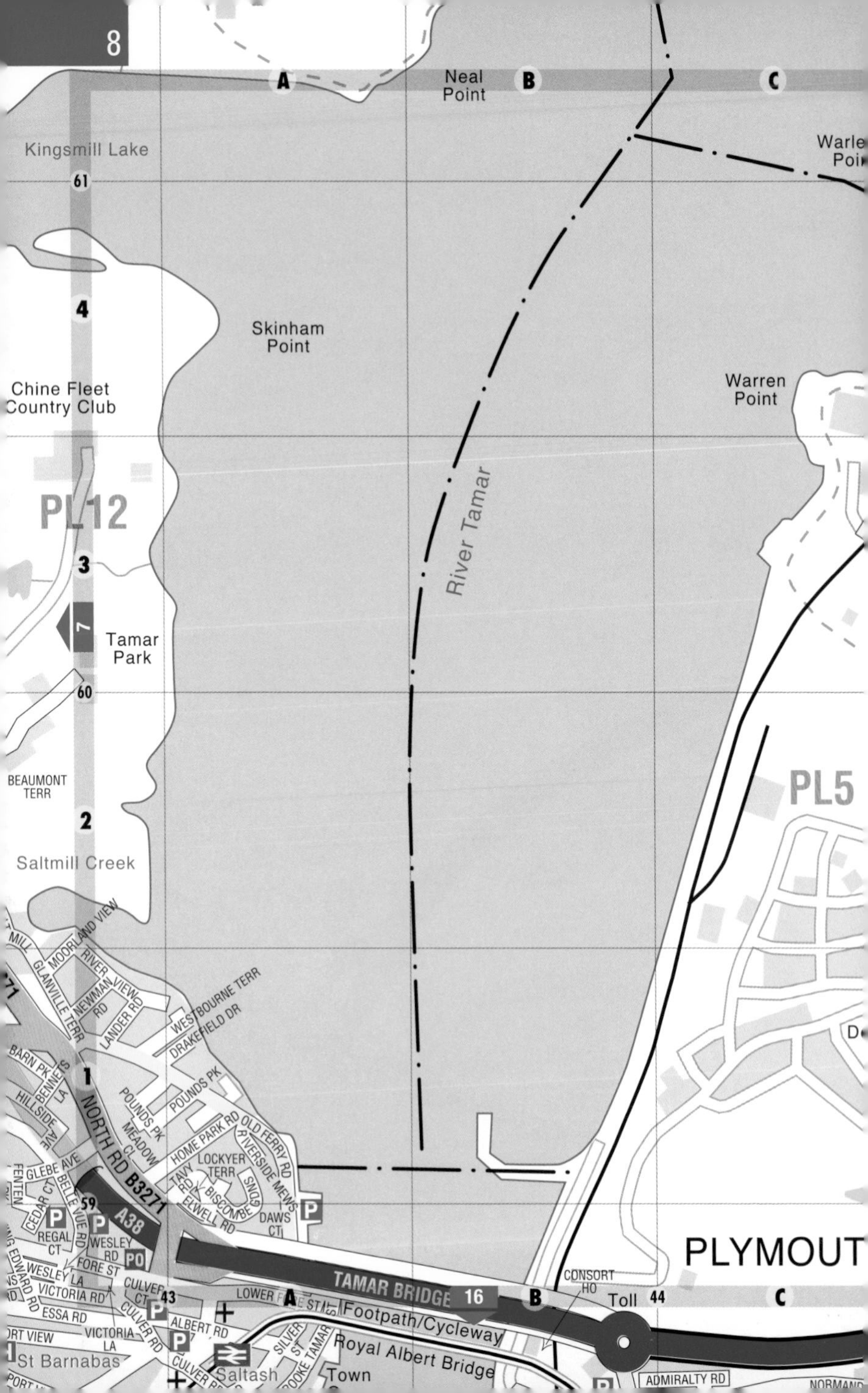

Neal Point
Kingsmill Lake
Skinham Point
Chine Fleet Country Club
PL12
River Tamar
Warren Point
Tamar Park
BEAUMONT TERR
Saltmill Creek
PL5
MOORLAND VIEW
RIVER VIEW
GLANVILLE TERR
NEWMAN RD
LANDER RD
WESTBOURNE TERR
DRAKEFIELD DR
BARN PK
BENNETS LA
HILLSIDE AVE
NORTH RD B3271
POUNDS PK
POUNDS PK MEADOW CL
HOME PARK RD
OLD FERRY RD
RIVERSIDE MEWS
LOCKYER TERR
TAVY RD
BISCOMBE GDNS
ELWELL RD
DAWS CT
GLEBE AVE
FENTEN
CEDAR CT
BELLE VUE RD
A38
REGAL CT
WESLEY RD
PO
FORE ST
WESLEY LA
VICTORIA RD
ESSA RD
CULVER CT
CULVER RD
VICTORIA LA
ALBERT RD
LOWER FORE ST
TAMAR BRIDGE
16
Footpath/Cycleway
Royal Albert Bridge
SILVER ST
BROOKE TAMAR
Saltash
Town
St Barnabas
CONSORT HO
Toll
PLYMOUT
ADMIRALTY RD

Tavy Bridge
Warleigh Wood
Reedwell Plantation
PL5
Tor Plantation
Tor Rock
Woodlands House
Badgers Park Wood
amarton Bridge
STATION RD
LAKESIDE DR
MANSTON CL
DIGBY GR
TANGMERE AVE
WEALD GDNS
NORTH
CATTERICK CL
WEST MALLING AVE
Liby
DUXFORD CL
HORNCHURCH RD
HORNCHURCH LA
ERNESETTLE GN
WARMWELL RD
STAPLEFORD GDNS
ROCHFORD CRES
MANBY GDNS
HILL PATH
LYMPNE AVE
WESTHAMPNETT PL
BIGGIN HILL
RUSSET WOOD
Budshead Creek
CAMBORNE CL
REDRUTH CL
TRURO DR
HOLLY PARK CL
DRAKE CT
UXBRIDGE DR
NORTHOLT AVE
CHIVENOR AVE
EXETER CL
MIDDLETON WLK
GRAVESEND WLK
DEBDEN CL
MAIDSTONE PL
CROYDON GDNS
ST EVAL PL
MARTLESHAM PL
KENLEY GDNS
Mill Ford Sch
COLTISHALL CL
Budshead Wood
HAWKINGE GDNS
ACKLINGTON PL
PEMBREY WLK
Ernesettle Jun & Inf Sch
YELVERTON CL
CULDROSE CL
REDHILL CL
PERRANPORTH CL
BUDSHEAD RD
ANZAC AVE
VALIANT AVE
RAMILLIES AVE
MARINA RD
QUEENS RD
KINGS RD
JUBILEE RD
PARADE RD
RINGMORE WAY
BELSTONE CL
PRINCESS AVE
ERNESETTLE LA
Playing Field
Ernesettle
THE GREEN
KINSALE RD
CROWNHILL RD
B3413
ERNESETTLE CRES
Ernesettle Battery
MARETT RD
DUNSTONE RD
WOLLATON GR
CHATSWORTH GDNS
HIRMANDALE RD
SHERFORD CRES
KEDLESTONE AVE
COOMBE PK
West Park
DUNCOMBE AVE
EASTBURY AVE
WANSTEAD
THE PARKWAY
AGATON RD
ERNESETTLE RD
DALTON GDNS
PRIESTLEY AVE
PLAISTOW CL
St Budeaux Foundation CE Jun Sch
BUCKINGHAM PL
CREST RD
NEWMAN RD
MOLLISON RD
HILL TOP
ROMAN WAY
STEPHENSON WAY
A38
esettle Farm
BICKHAM RD
PLAISTOW CRES
Mount Tamar Sch
ROW LA
King's Tamerton
HOWARD CL
KING'S TAMERTON
WAVERLEY RD
VICTORIA RD
VERNA PL
CHARD RD
CLIFFORD
NEWTON AVE
CAYLEY WAY
A
B
C
1
2
3
4
45
46
59
60
61
10
17

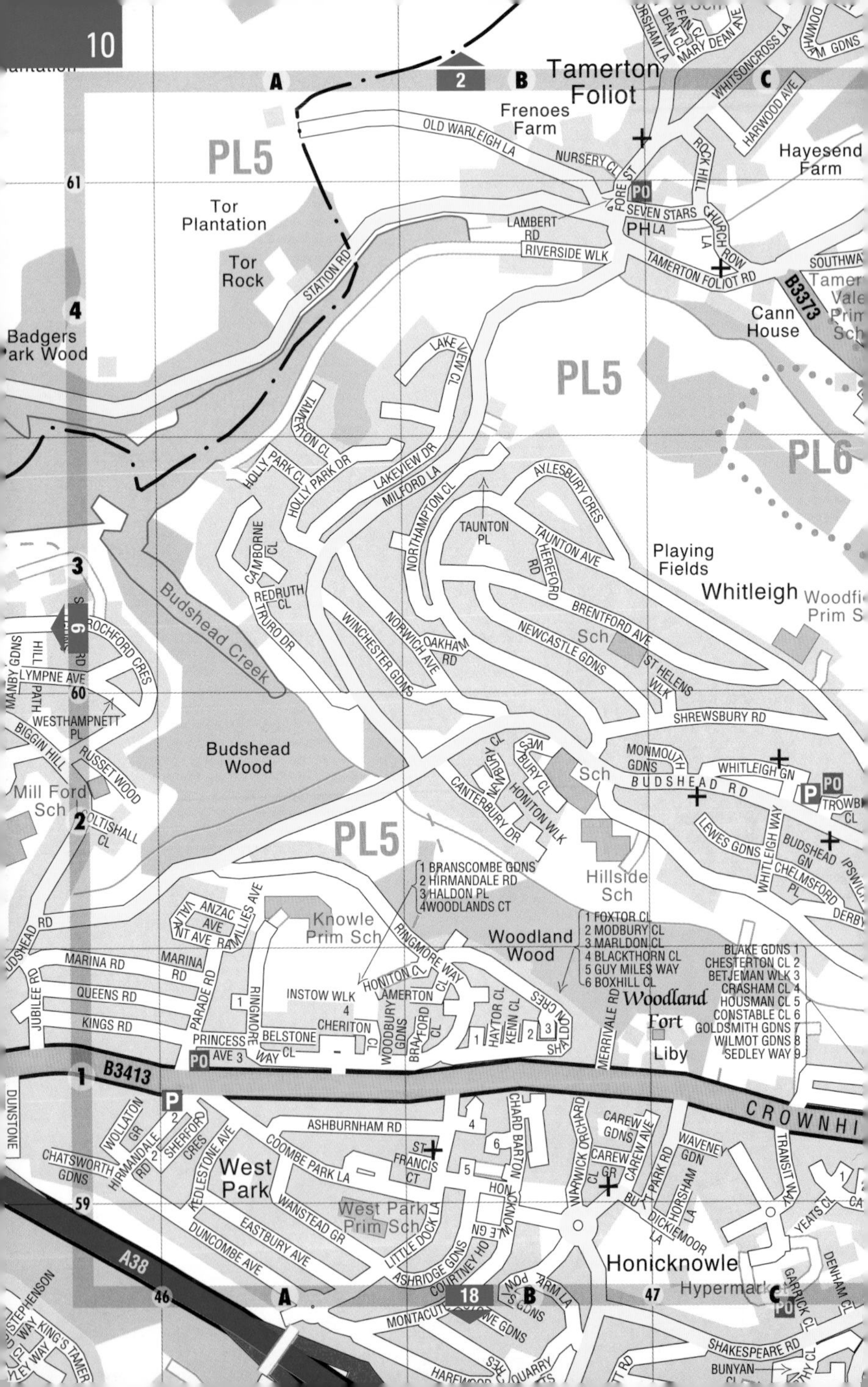

Tamerton Foliot
Frenoes Farm
Hayesend Farm
PL5
Tor Plantation
Tor Rock
Badgers Park Wood
Cann House
PL5
PL6
Playing Fields
Whitleigh
Budshead Creek
Budshead Wood
Mill Ford Sch
PL5
Knowle Prim Sch
Hillside Sch
Woodland Wood
Woodland Fort
Liby
West Park
West Park Prim Sch
Honicknowle
Hypermarket
1 BRANSCOMBE GDNS
2 HIRMANDALE RD
3 HALDON PL
4 WOODLANDS CT
1 FOXTOR CL
2 MODBURY CL
3 MARLDON CL
4 BLACKTHORN CL
5 GUY MILES WAY
6 BOXHILL CL
BLAKE GDNS 1
CHESTERTON CL 2
BETJEMAN WLK 3
CRASHAM CL 4
HOUSMAN CL 5
CONSTABLE CL 6
GOLDSMITH GDNS 7
WILMOT GDNS 8
SEDLEY WAY 9
B3413
B3373
A38
CROWNHI

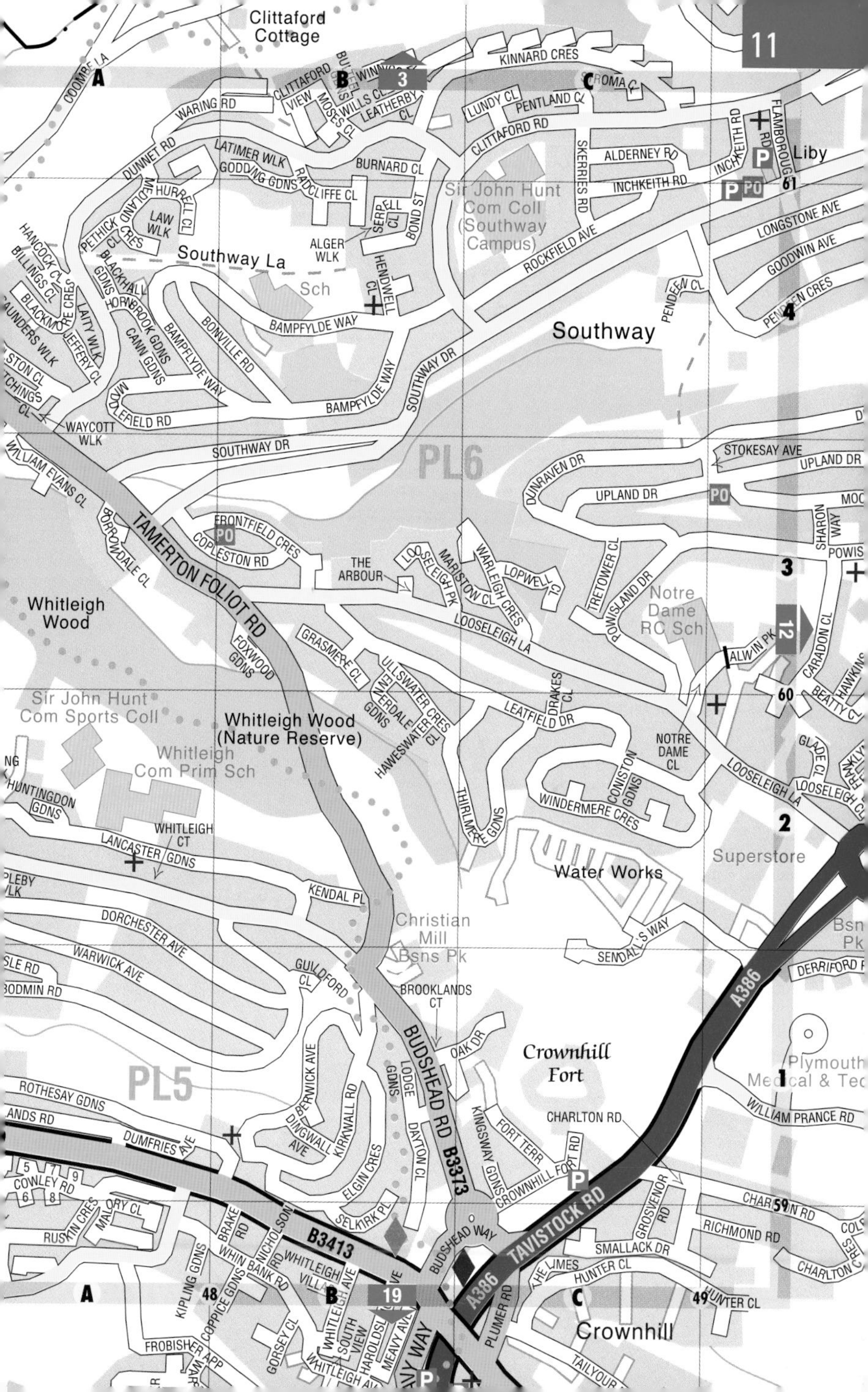
Clittaford Cottage
COOMBE LA
A
B
C
3
KINNARD CRES
CLITTAFORD VIEW
WINNOW CL
WILLS CL
LEATHERBY CL
MOSES CL
LUNDY CL
PENTLAND CL
CLITTAFORD RD
WARING RD
DUNNET RD
LATIMER WLK
GODDING GDNS
RADCLIFFE CL
BURNARD CL
HURRELL CL
MEDLAND CRES
LAW WLK
SERPELL CL
BOND ST
ALGER WLK
HENDWELL CL
Sir John Hunt Com Coll (Southway Campus)
ALDERNEY RD
SKERRIES RD
INCHKEITH RD
FLAMBOROUGH RD
Liby
61
LONGSTONE AVE
GOODWIN AVE
PENDEEN CRES
PENDEEN CL
4
ROCKFIELD AVE
Southway La
Sch
HANCOCK CL
BILLINGS CL
BLACKMORE CRES
LAITY WLK
JEFFERY CL
SAUNDERS WLK
PETHICK CL
BLACKHALL GDNS
HORNBROOK GDNS
CANN GDNS
BAMPFYLDE WAY
BONVILLE RD
MIDDLEFIELD RD
Southway
SOUTHWAY DR
WAYCOTT WLK
PL6
WILLIAM EVANS CL
BORROWDALE CL
TAMERTON FOLIOT RD
FRONTFIELD CRES
COPLESTON RD
PO
THE ARBOUR
LOOSELEIGH PK
MARISTOW CL
WARLEIGH CRES
LOPWELL CL
DUNRAVEN DR
UPLAND DR
STOKESAY AVE
SHARON WAY
POWIS
3
TRETOWER CL
POWISLAND DR
Notre Dame RC Sch
12
ALWIN PK
CARADON CL
HAWKINS
BEATTY CL
60
Whitleigh Wood
LOOSELEIGH LA
GRASMERE CL
ULLSWATER CRES
ENNERDALE GDNS
FOXWOOD GDNS
LEATFIELD DR
DRAKES CL
NOTRE DAME CL
Sir John Hunt Com Sports Coll
Whitleigh Wood (Nature Reserve)
HAWESWATER CL
Whitleigh Com Prim Sch
HUNTINGDON GDNS
THIRLMERE GDNS
CONISTON GDNS
WINDERMERE CRES
GLADE CL
2
Superstore
WHITLEIGH CT
LANCASTER GDNS
KENDAL PL
Water Works
DORCHESTER AVE
Christian Mill Bsns Pk
SENDALLS WAY
DERRIFORD
WARWICK AVE
GUILDFORD CL
BODMIN RD
BROOKLANDS CT
A386
OAK DR
Crownhill Fort
PL5
BERWICK AVE
KIRKWALL RD
LODGE GDNS
BUDSHEAD RD B3373
Plymouth Medical & Tec
1
WILLIAM PRANCE RD
ROTHESAY GDNS
DINGWALL AVE
DAYTON CL
ELGIN CRES
KINGSWAY GDNS
FORT TERR
CHARLTON RD
CROWNHILL FORT RD
DUMFRIES AVE
COWLEY RD
TAVISTOCK RD
GROSVENOR RD
CHARLTON RD
59
RICHMOND RD
MALORY CL
RUSKIN CRES
BRAKE RD
NICHOLSON RD
B3413
SELKIRK PL
BUDSHEAD WAY
SMALLACK DR
CHARLTON CRES
WHIN BANK RD
WHITLEIGH VILLAS
THE LIMES
HUNTER CL
A
48
B
19
C
49
KIPLING GDNS
COPPICE GDNS
WHITLEIGH AVE
PLUMER RD
Crownhill
GORSEY CL
SOUTH VIEW
HAROLDSLEIGH AVE
MEAVY AVE
FROBISHER APP
TAILYOUR

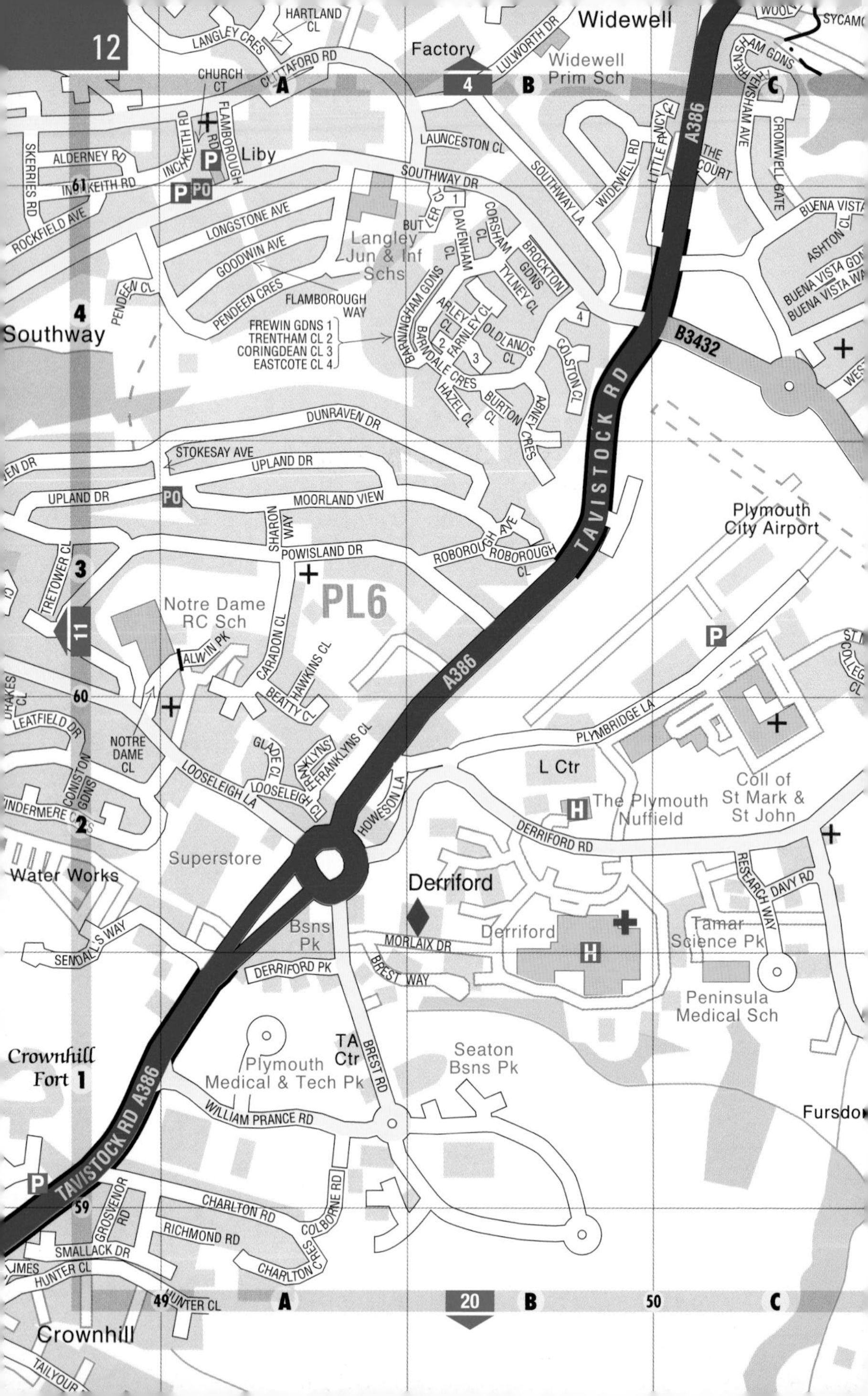
HARTLAND CL
LANGLEY CRES
CUTTAFORD RD
CHURCH CT
A
Factory
4
LULWORTH DR
Widewell
Widewell Prim Sch
B
WOOL
SYCAMO
HENSHAM GDNS
HENSHAM AVE
C
CROMWELL GATE
THE COURT
A386
LITTLE FANCY CL
WIDEWELL RD
SOUTHWAY LA
LAUNCESTON CL
SOUTHWAY DR
FLAMBOROUGH RD
KEITH RD
INCHKEITH RD
Liby
P
PO
SKERRIES RD
ALDERNEY RD
61
ROCKFIELD AVE
LONGSTONE AVE
GOODWIN AVE
PENDEEN CRES
PENDEEN CL
Langley Jun & Inf Schs
BUTLER CL
DAVENHAM CL
CORSHAM CL
BROCKTON GDNS
TYLNEY CL
BUENA VISTA
ASHTON CL
BUENA VISTA GDNS
BUENA VISTA WAY
FLAMBOROUGH WAY
FREWIN GDNS 1
TRENTHAM CL 2
CORINGDEAN CL 3
EASTCOTE CL 4
BARNINGHAM GDNS
ARLEY CL
FARNLEY CL
OLDLANDS CL
COLSTON CL
BARNDALE CRES
HAZEL CL
BURTON CL
ABNEY CRES
B3432
WEST
4
Southway
DUNRAVEN DR
STOKESAY AVE
UPLAND DR
MOORLAND VIEW
SHARON WAY
POWISLAND DR
ROBOROUGH AVE
ROBOROUGH CL
TAVISTOCK RD
Plymouth City Airport
TRETOWER CL
3
11
Notre Dame RC Sch
ALWIN PK
PL6
CARADON CL
HAWKINS CL
BEATTY CL
A386
P
ST
COLLEGE CL
DRAKES CL
60
LEATFIELD DR
NOTRE DAME CL
GLADE CL
FRANKLYNS
FRANKLYNS CL
PLYMBRIDGE LA
L Ctr
Coll of St Mark & St John
CONISTON GDNS
WINDERMERE CRES
2
LOOSELEIGH LA
LOOSELEIGH CL
HOWESON LA
H
The Plymouth Nuffield
DERRIFORD RD
Superstore
Water Works
Derriford
RESEARCH WAY
DAVY RD
SENDALL'S WAY
Bsns Pk
MORLAIX DR
Derriford
H
Tamar Science Pk
DERRIFORD PK
BREST WAY
Peninsula Medical Sch
Crownhill Fort
1
TA Ctr
BREST RD
Plymouth Medical & Tech Pk
Seaton Bsns Pk
TAVISTOCK RD A386
WILLIAM PRANCE RD
Fursdon
P
59
GROSVENOR RD
CHARLTON RD
COLBORNE RD
RICHMOND RD
SMALLACK DR
CHARLTON CRES
JAMES
HUNTER CL
49
HUNTER CL
A
20
B
50
C
Crownhill
TAILYOUR

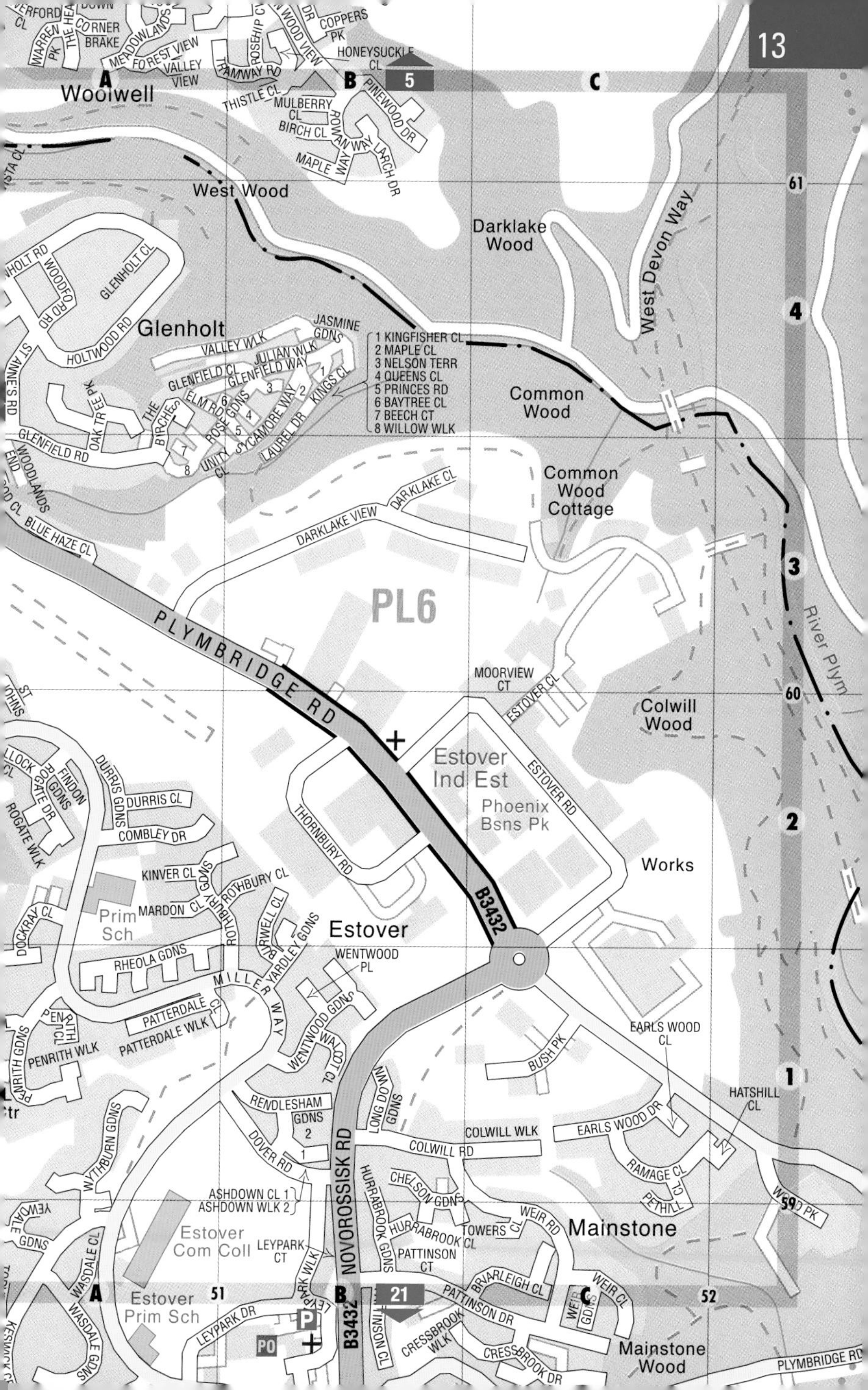

Woolwell
West Wood
Darklake Wood
West Devon Way
Glenholt
Common Wood
Common Wood Cottage
PL6
PLYMBRIDGE RD
Colwill Wood
River Plym
Estover Ind Est
Phoenix Bsns Pk
Works
Estover
B3432
Prim Sch
Mainstone
Estover Com Coll
Estover Prim Sch
Mainstone Wood
NOVOROSSISK RD
1 KINGFISHER CL
2 MAPLE CL
3 NELSON TERR
4 QUEENS CL
5 PRINCES RD
6 BAYTREE CL
7 BEECH CT
8 WILLOW WLK
ASHDOWN CL 1
ASHDOWN WLK 2
DARKLAKE VIEW
DARKLAKE CL
MOORVIEW CT
ESTOVER CL
ESTOVER RD
THORNBURY RD
HOLTWOOD RD
GLENHOLT CL
GLENHOLT RD
WOODFORD RD
ST ANNE'S RD
OAK TREE PK
GLENFIELD RD
GLENFIELD CL
GLENFIELD WAY
VALLEY WLK
JULIAN WLK
JASMINE GDNS
KINGS CL
LAUREL DR
SYCAMORE WAY
ROSE GDNS
ELM RD
UNITY CL
THE BIRCHES
BLUE HAZE CL
WOODLANDS END
MEADOWLANDS
FOREST VIEW
VALLEY VIEW
TRAMWAY RD
THISTLE CL
MULBERRY CL
BIRCH CL
MAPLE WAY
ROWAN WAY
LARCH DR
PINEWOOD DR
HONEYSUCKLE CL
COPPERS PK
CORNER BRAKE
DURRIS CL
DURRIS GDNS
COMBLEY DR
FINDON GDNS
ROGATE DR
ROGATE WLK
KINVER CL
ROTHBURY CL
ROTHBURY GDNS
MARDON CL
BURWELL CL
YARDLEY GDNS
DOCKRAY CL
RHEOLA GDNS
MILLER WAY
PATTERDALE CL
PATTERDALE WLK
PENRITH CL
PENRITH WLK
PENRITH GDNS
WENTWOOD PL
WENTWOOD GDNS
WALCOT CL
RENDLESHAM GDNS
DOVER RD
WYTHBURN GDNS
WASDALE CL
WASDALE GDNS
YEWDALE GDNS
LEYPARK CT
LEYPARK WLK
LEYPARK DR
LONG DOWN GDNS
BUSH PK
EARLS WOOD CL
EARLS WOOD DR
HATSHILL CL
COLWILL WLK
COLWILL RD
RAMAGE CL
PETHILL CL
WOOD PK
HURRABROOK CL
HURRABROOK GDNS
CHELSON GDNS
TOWERS CL
WEIR RD
WEIR CL
WEIR GDNS
PATTINSON CT
PATTINSON DR
PATTINSON CL
BRIARLEIGH CL
CRESSBROOK WLK
CRESSBROOK DR
PLYMBRIDGE RD
A
B
C
5
21
1
2
3
4
51
52
59
60
61

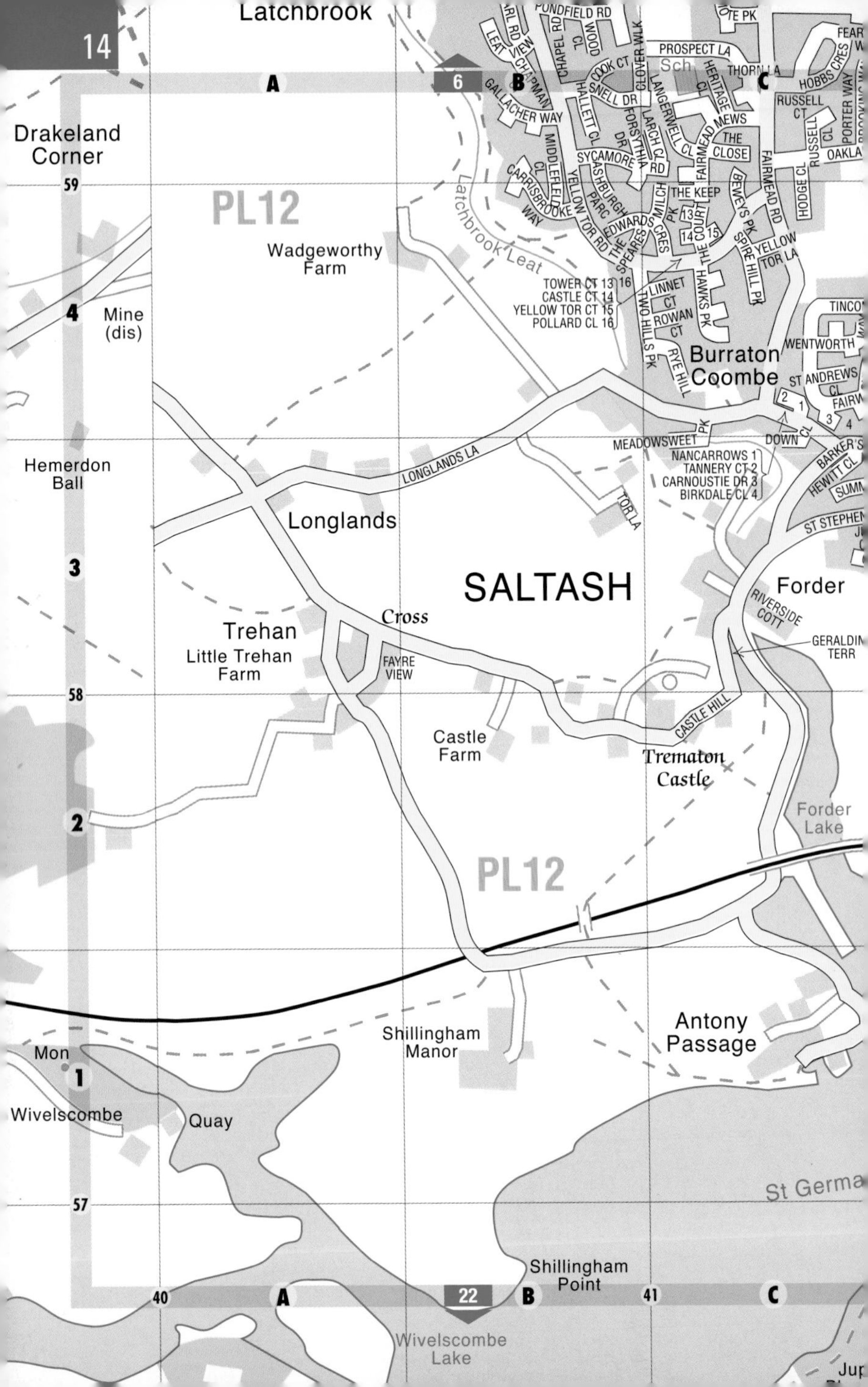
Latchbrook
Drakeland Corner
PL12
Wadgeworthy Farm
Latchbrook Leat
Mine (dis)
Hemerdon Ball
Longlands
LONGLANDS LA
SALTASH
Trehan
Little Trehan Farm
Cross
FAYRE VIEW
Castle Farm
CASTLE HILL
Trematon Castle
Forder
RIVERSIDE COTT
GERALDINE TERR
Forder Lake
PL12
Burraton Coombe
TOWER CT 13
CASTLE CT 14
YELLOW TOR CT 15
POLLARD CL 16
NANCARROWS 1
TANNERY CT 2
CARNOUSTIE DR 3
BIRKDALE CL 4
MEADOWSWEET PK
DOWN CL
TOR LA
PROSPECT LA
THORN LA
HOBBS CRES
RUSSELL CT
RUSSELL CL
PORTER WAY
FAIRMEAD RD
HODGE CL
YELLOW TOR LA
WENTWORTH
ST ANDREWS CL
ST STEPHENS
Antony Passage
Shillingham Manor
Mon
Wivelscombe
Quay
St Germans
Shillingham Point
Wivelscombe Lake
A
B
C
6
22
40
41
57
58
59
1
2
3
4

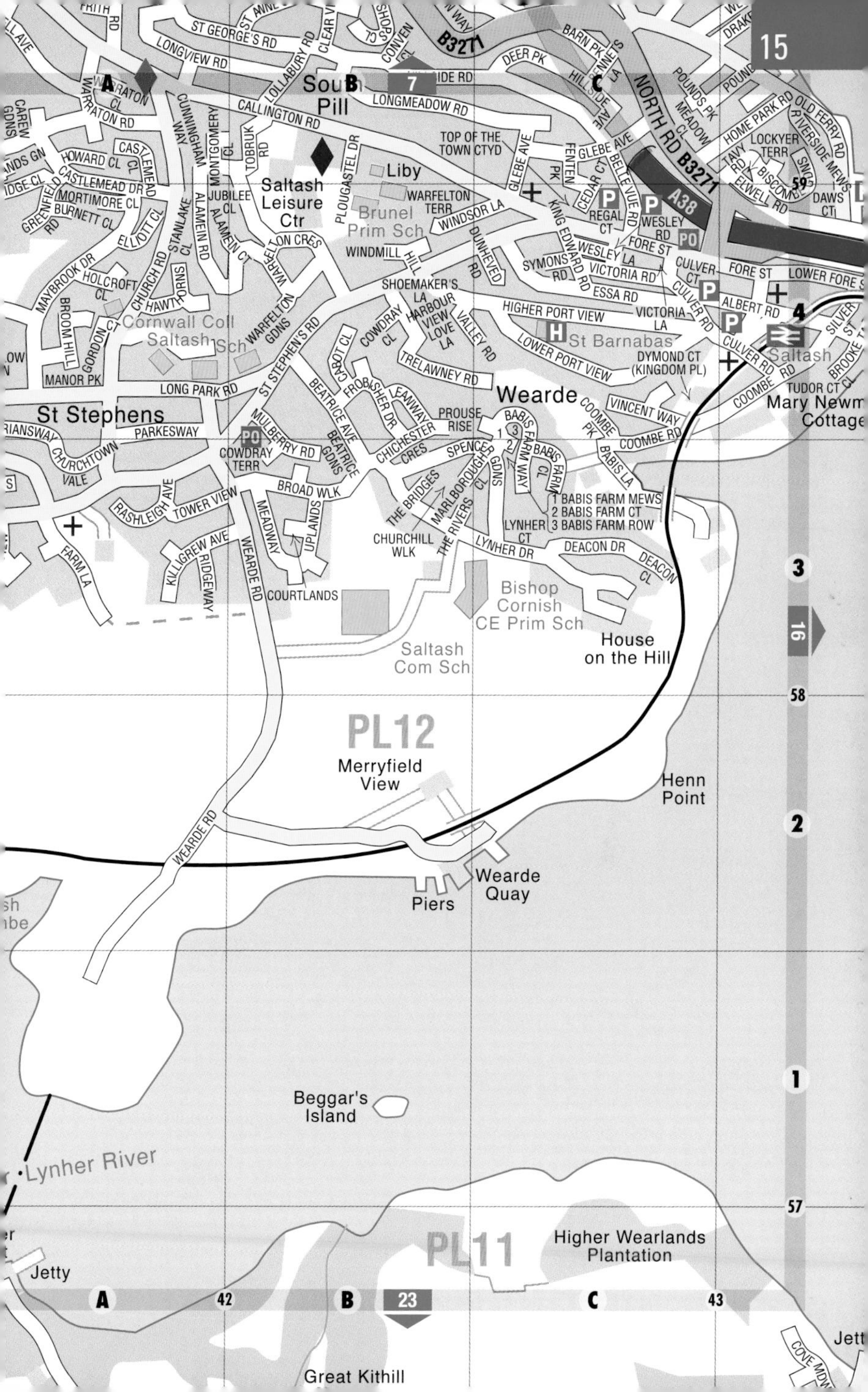

South Pill
Saltash Leisure Ctr
Liby
Brunel Prim Sch
Cornwall Coll Saltash Sch
St Stephens
Wearde
St Barnabas
Saltash
Mary Newman Cottage
Bishop Cornish CE Prim Sch
Saltash Com Sch
House on the Hill
PL12
Merryfield View
Henn Point
Wearde Quay
Piers
Beggar's Island
Lynher River
PL11
Higher Wearlands Plantation
Jetty
Great Kithill
NORTH RD B3271
A38
B3271
CALLINGTON RD
LONGMEADOW RD
LONGVIEW RD
ST GEORGE'S RD
LONG PARK RD
ST STEPHEN'S RD
WEARDE RD
LYNHER DR
DEACON DR
COOMBE RD
HIGHER PORT VIEW
LOWER PORT VIEW
FORE ST
LOWER FORE ST
CULVER RD
VICTORIA RD
ESSA RD
ALBERT RD
WINDSOR LA
TRELAWNEY RD
PARKESWAY
CHURCHTOWN VALE
TOWER VIEW
RASHLEIGH AVE
KILLIGREW AVE
RIDGEWAY
MEADWAY
UPLANDS
COURTLANDS
BROAD WLK
MULBERRY RD
COWDRAY TERR
BEATRICE AVE
BEATRICE GDNS
CHICHESTER CRES
FROBISHER DR
LEANWAY
PROUSE RISE
SPENCER GDNS
MARLBOROUGH CL
THE BRIDGES
THE RIVERS
CHURCHILL WLK
LYNHER CT
BABIS FARM WAY
BABIS FARM CL
BABIS LA
1 BABIS FARM MEWS
2 BABIS FARM CT
3 BABIS FARM ROW
VINCENT WAY
DYMOND CT (KINGDOM PL)
MANOR PK
BROOM HILL
GORDON CT
MAYBROOK DR
HOLCROFT CL
HAWTHORNS
CHURCH RD
STANLAKE CL
ALAMEIN RD
ALAMEIN CT
JUBILEE CL
WARFELTON CRES
WARFELTON GDNS
WARFELTON TERR
PLOUGASTEL DR
WINDMILL HILL
SHOEMAKER'S LA
HARBOUR VIEW
LOVE LA
VALLEY RD
DUNHEVED RD
GLEBE AVE
KING EDWARD RD
SYMONS RD
WESLEY LA
WESLEY RD
REGAL CT
CEDAR CT
BELLE VUE RD
FENTEN PK
TOP OF THE TOWN CTYD
HILLSIDE AVE
DEER PK
BARN PK
BENNETS LA
POUNDS PK
MEADOW CL
HOME PARK RD
OLD FERRY RD
RIVERSIDE MEWS
LOCKYER TERR
TAVY RD
ELWELL RD
DAWS CT
CULVER CT
TUDOR CT
COOMBE PK
FARM LA
WARRATON CL
WARRATON RD
CAREW GDNS
HOWARD CL
CASTLEMEAD CL
CASTLEMEAD DR
MORTIMORE CL
BURNETT CL
ELLIOTT CL
GREENFIELD RD
CUNNINGHAM WAY
MONTGOMERY CL
TOBRUK RD
LOLLABURY RD
CLEAR VIEW
CONVENT CL
ST ANNE'S
FRITH RD
SILVER ST
BROOKE
COVE MDW
A
B
C
42
43
57
58
59
1
2
3
4
7
16
23

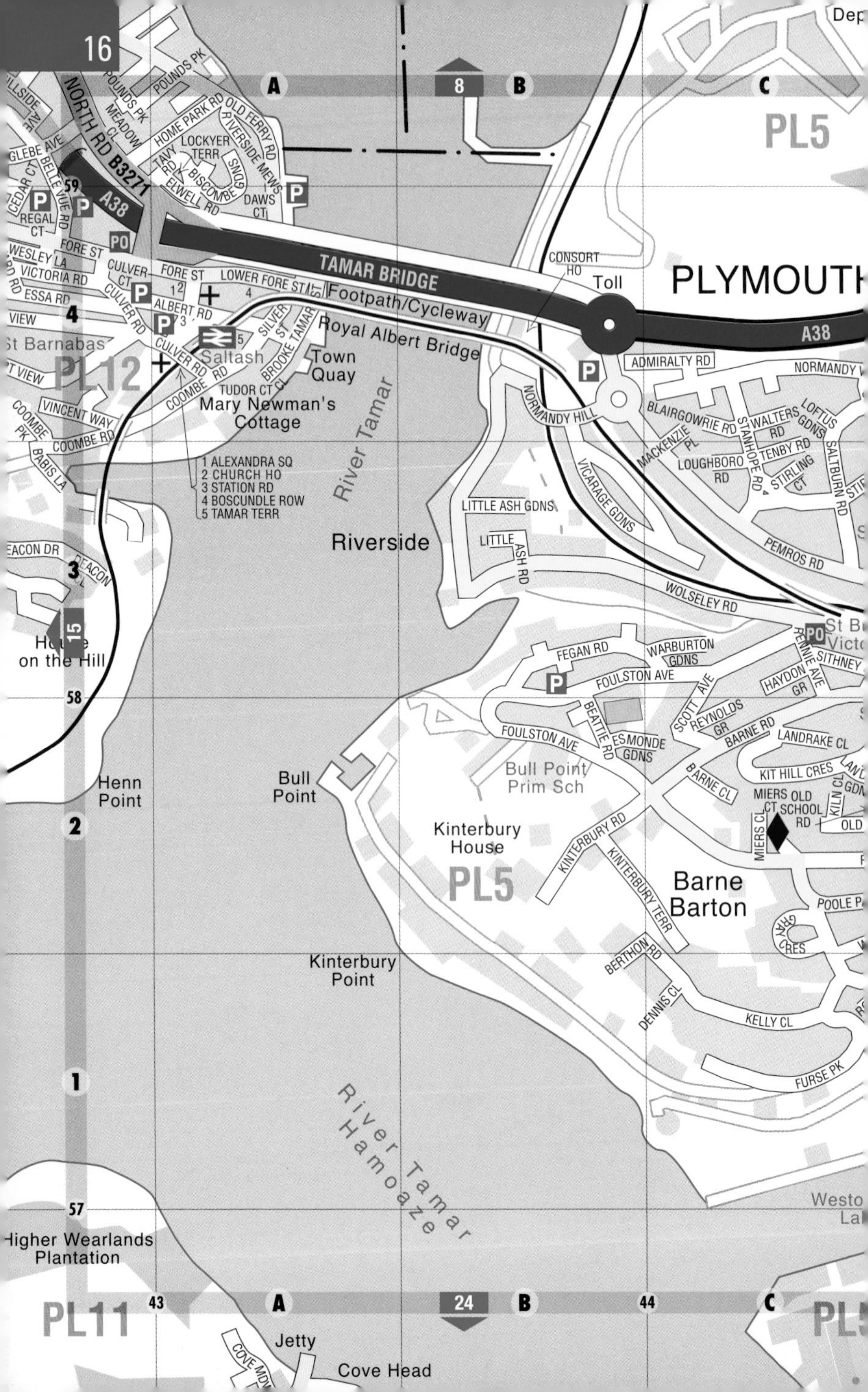
PL5
PLYMOUTH
TAMAR BRIDGE
A38
B3271
NORTH RD
Footpath/Cycleway
Royal Albert Bridge
Toll
CONSORT HO
Saltash
PL12
St Barnabas
Town Quay
Mary Newman's Cottage
River Tamar
Riverside
1 ALEXANDRA SQ
2 CHURCH HO
3 STATION RD
4 BOSCUNDLE ROW
5 TAMAR TERR
POUNDS PK
HOME PARK RD
OLD FERRY RD
RIVERSIDE MEWS
LOCKYER TERR
TAVY RD
BISCOMBE GDNS
ELWELL RD
DAWS CT
GLEBE AVE
BELLE VUE RD
CEDAR CT
REGAL CT
FORE ST
WESLEY LA
VICTORIA RD
ESSA RD
CULVER CT
CULVER RD
LOWER FORE ST
ALBERT RD
SILVER ST
BROOKE TAMAR
TUDOR CT
COOMBE RD
VINCENT WAY
COOMBE PK
BABIS LA
DEACON DR
DEACON CL
House on the Hill
Henn Point
Bull Point
Kinterbury House
Kinterbury Point
River Tamar Hamoaze
Higher Wearlands Plantation
PL11
Jetty
Cove Head
ADMIRALTY RD
NORMANDY HILL
BLAIRGOWRIE RD
MACKENZIE PL
STANHOPE RD
WALTERS RD
LOFTUS GDNS
TENBY RD
LOUGHBORO RD
STIRLING CT
SALTBURN RD
VICARAGE GDNS
LITTLE ASH GDNS
LITTLE ASH RD
PEMROS RD
WOLSELEY RD
FEGAN RD
WARBURTON GDNS
FOULSTON AVE
SCOTT AVE
REYNOLDS GR
HAYDON GR
RENNIE AVE
SITHNEY
BEATTIE RD
ESMONDE GDNS
BARNE RD
LANDRAKE CL
KIT HILL CRES
BARNE CL
Bull Point Prim Sch
MIERS CT
MIERS CL
OLD SCHOOL RD
KILN CL
KINTERBURY RD
KINTERBURY TERR
Barne Barton
POOLE PK
GRAY CRES
BERTHON RD
DENNIS CL
KELLY CL
FURSE PK
8
24
15
A
B
C
43
44
57
58
59

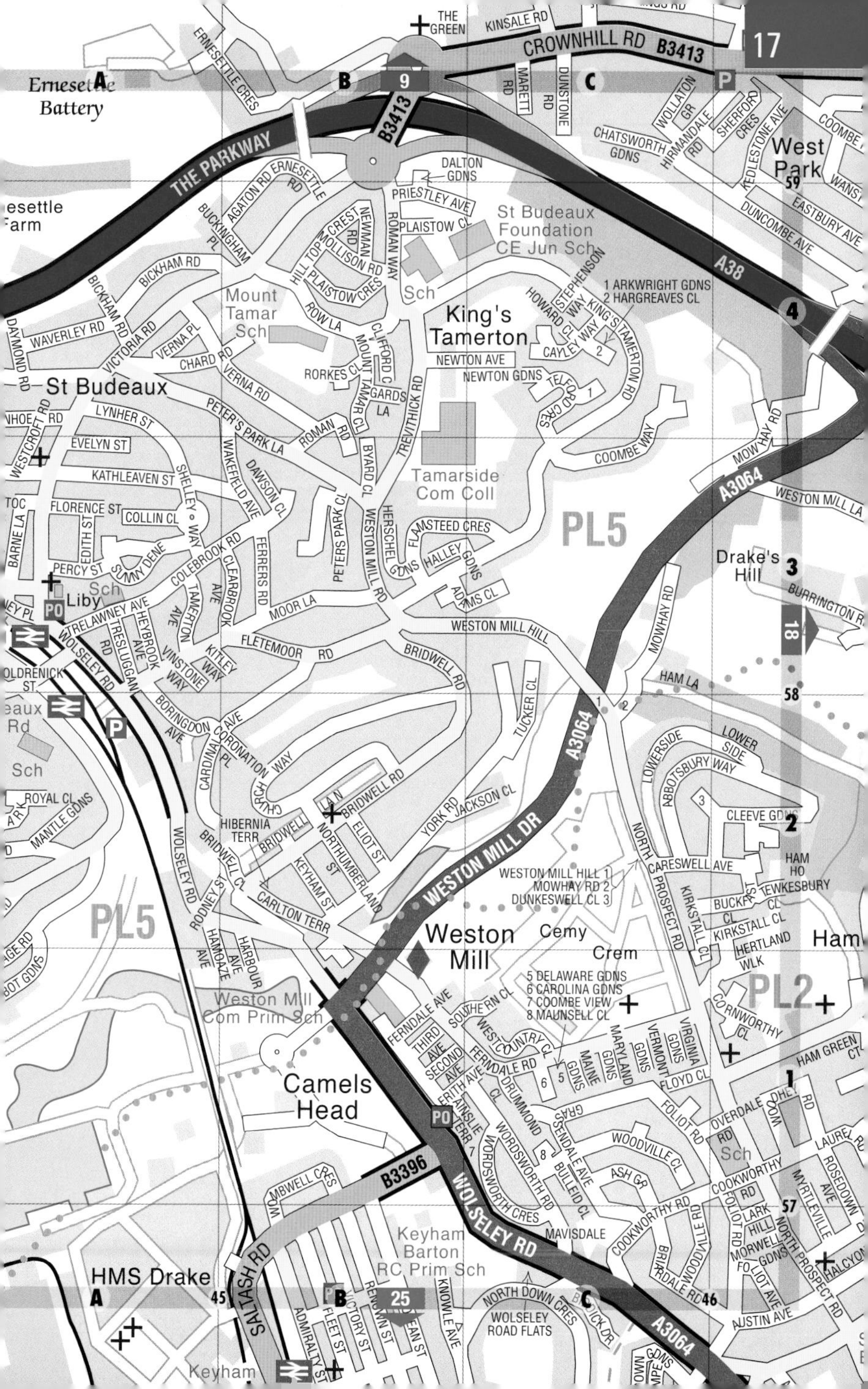

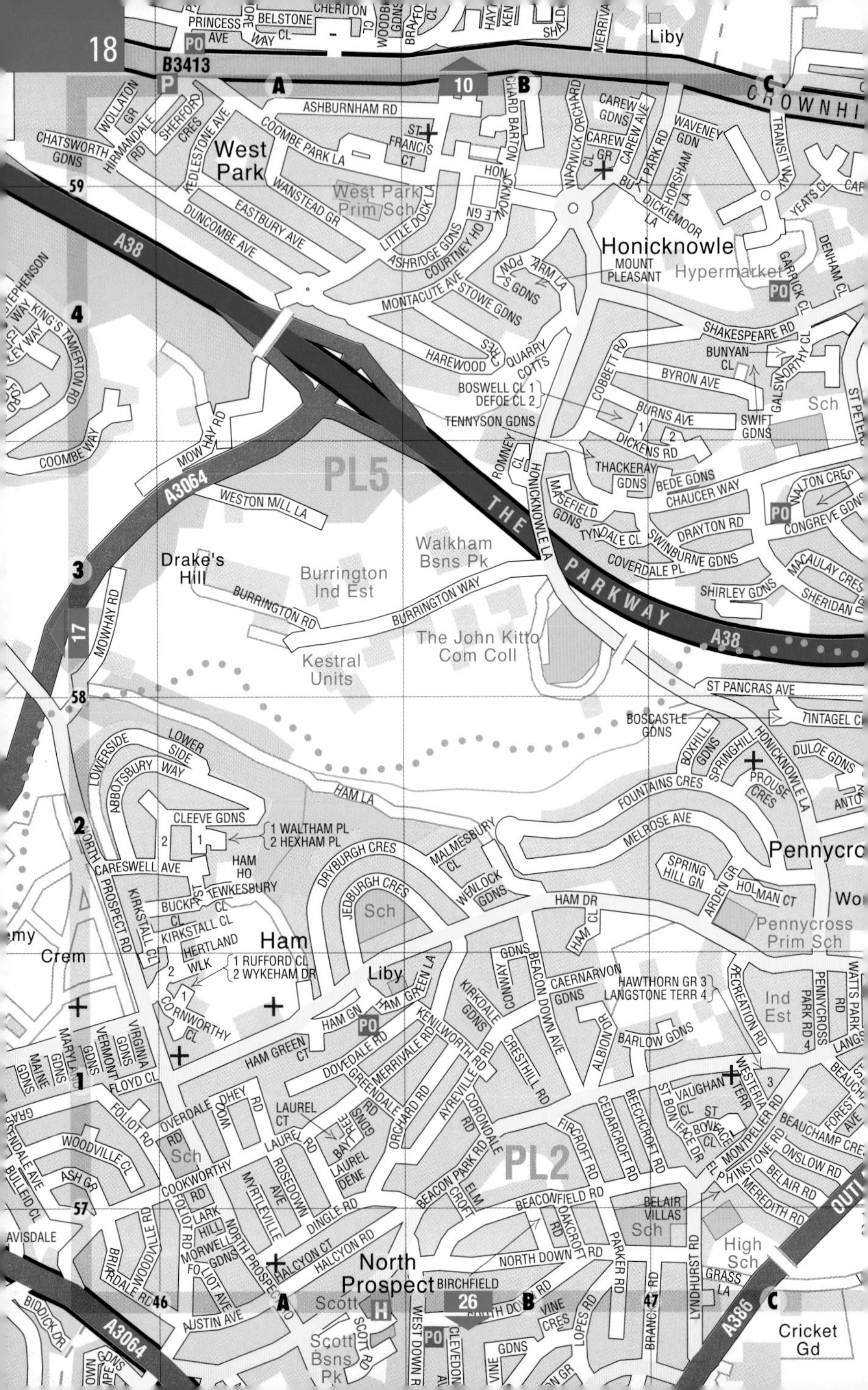

18
B3413
A
10
B
C
CROWNHILL
West Park
Honicknowle
Hypermarket
ASHBURNHAM RD
COOMBE PARK LA
ST FRANCIS CT
West Park Prim Sch
WANSTEAD GR
EASTBURY AVE
DUNCOMBE AVE
KEDLESTONE AVE
SHERFORD CRES
HIRMANDALE RD
WOLLATON GR
CHATSWORTH GDNS
59
A38
LITTLE DOCK LA
ASHRIDGE GDNS
COURTNEY HO
MONTACUTE AVE
STOWE GDNS
HAREWOOD CRES
QUARRY COTTS
ORCHARD BARTON
WARWICK ORCHARD CL
CAREW GDNS
CAREW GR
CAREW AVE
BUTT PARK RD
WAVENEY GDN
HORSHAM LA
DICKIEMOOR LA
TRANSIT WAY
YEATS CL
GARRICK CL
DENHAM CL
MOUNT PLEASANT
SHAKESPEARE RD
BUNYAN CL
COBBETT RD
BYRON AVE
GALSWORTHY CL
Sch
BOSWELL CL 1
DEFOE CL 2
TENNYSON GDNS
BURNS AVE
SWIFT GDNS
DICKENS RD
THACKERAY GDNS
BEDE GDNS
CHAUCER WAY
WALTON CRES
CONGREVE GDNS
MASEFIELD GDNS
TYNDALE CL
DRAYTON RD
SWINBURNE GDNS
COVERDALE PL
MACAULAY CRES
SHIRLEY GDNS
SHERIDAN
ROMNEY CL
HONICKNOWLE LA
THE PARKWAY
PL5
STEPHENSON WAY
KING'S TAMERTON RD
4
COOMBE WAY
MOW HAY RD
A3064
WESTON MILL LA
Drake's Hill
Burrington Ind Est
Walkham Bsns Pk
BURRINGTON RD
BURRINGTON WAY
3
17
MOWHAY RD
Kestral Units
The John Kitto Com Coll
58
ST PANCRAS AVE
TINTAGEL CL
BOSCASTLE GDNS
BOXHILL GDNS
SPRINGHILL
DULOE GDNS
PROUSE CRES
FOUNTAINS CRES
MELROSE AVE
Pennycross
LOWERSIDE
LOWER SIDE
ABBOTSBURY WAY
HAM LA
CLEEVE GDNS
1 WALTHAM PL
2 HEXHAM PL
2
NORTH PROSPECT RD
CARESWELL AVE
HAM HO
TEWKESBURY CL
BUCKFAST CL
KIRKSTALL CL
HERTLAND WLK
DRYBURGH CRES
JEDBURGH CRES
MALMESBURY CL
WENLOCK GDNS
Sch
HAM DR
HAM CL
SPRING HILL GN
ARDEN GR
HOLMAN CT
Pennycross Prim Sch
Crem
Ham
1 RUFFORD CL
2 WYKEHAM DR
CORNWORTHY CL
Liby
HAM GREEN LA
HAM GN
HAM GREEN CT
CONWAY GDNS
KIRKDALE GDNS
BEACON DOWN AVE
CAERNARVON GDNS
HAWTHORN GR 3
LANGSTONE TERR 4
RECREATION RD
PENNYCROSS PARK RD
WATTS PARK RD
Ind Est
ALBION DR
BARLOW GDNS
VIRGINIA GDNS
VERMONT GDNS
MARYLAND GDNS
MAINE GDNS
1
FLOYD CL
FOLIOT RD
WOODVILLE CL
ASH GR
BULLEID CL
57
OVERDALE RD
WOODHEY RD
DOVEDALE RD
MERRIVALE RD
GREENDALE
KENILWORTH RD
LAUREL CT
LAUREL RD
BAYTREE GDNS
LAUREL DENE
ORCHARD RD
AYREVILLE RD
CORONDALE RD
CRESTHILL RD
FIRCROFT RD
CEDARCROFT RD
BEECHCROFT RD
ST BONIFACE DR
VAUGHAN CL
ST BONIFACE CL
WESTERIA TERR
MONTPELIER RD
BEAUCHAMP CRES
ONSLOW RD
PHINSTONE RD
BELAIR RD
MEREDITH RD
COOKWORTHY RD
ROSEDOWN AVE
MYRTLEVILLE
DINGLE RD
PL2
BEACON PARK RD
ELM CROFT
BEACONFIELD RD
OAKCROFT RD
BELAIR VILLAS
Sch
High Sch
LARK HILL
MORWELL GDNS
FOLIOT AVE
WOODVILLE RD
BRIARDALE RD
HALCYON CT
HALCYON RD
NORTH DOWN RD
PARKER RD
LYNDHURST RD
GRASS LA
A386
North Prospect
BIRCHFIELD
26
SOUTH DOWN RD
VINE CRES
LOPES RD
BRANCH RD
47
46
Scott
SCOTT RD
Scott Bsns Pk
AUSTIN AVE
BIDDICK DR
WEST DOWN RD
CLEVEDON
VINE GDNS
Cricket Gd

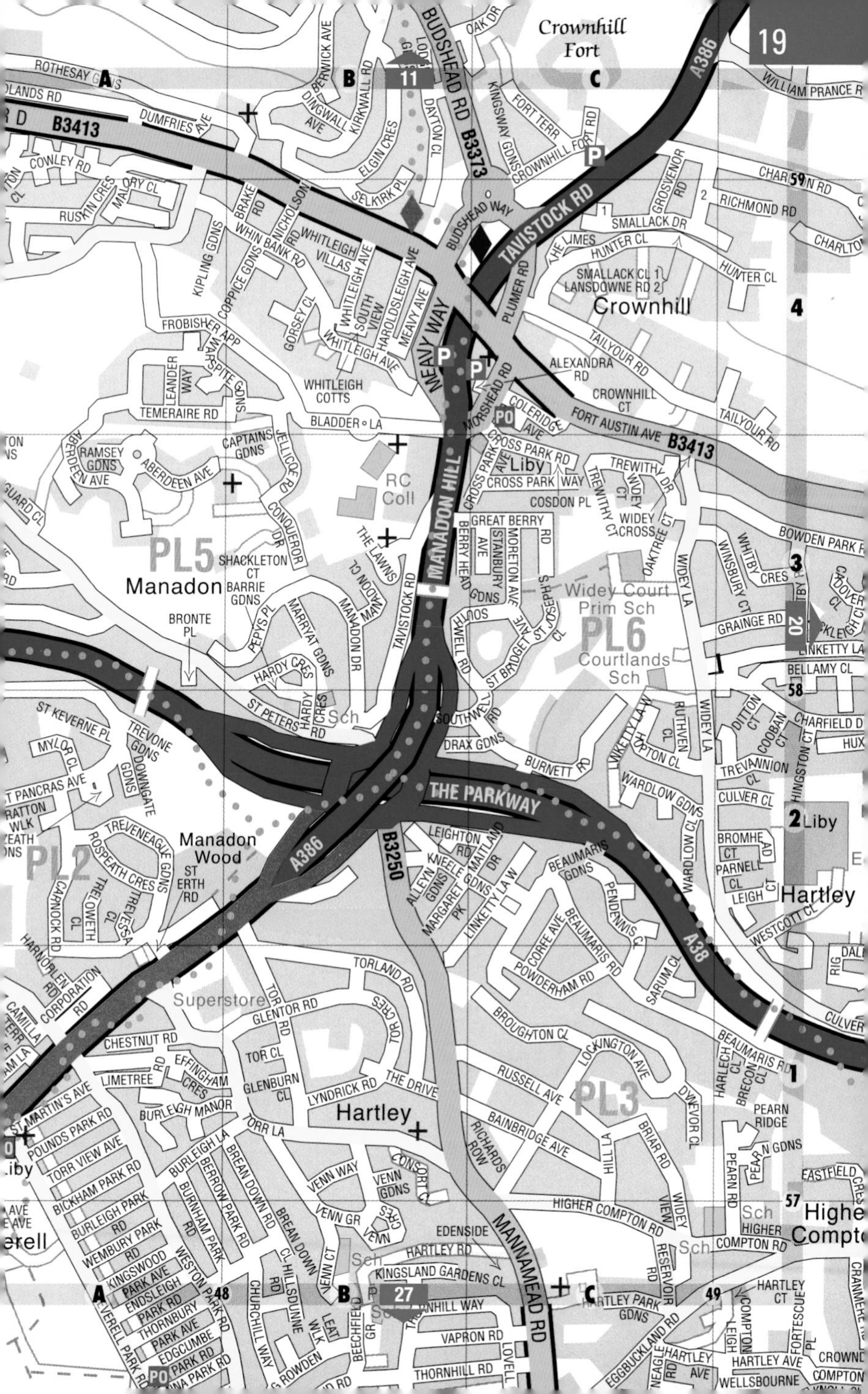
Crownhill Fort
A386
WILLIAM PRANCE RD
ROTHESAY GDNS
A
B
11
C
BUDSHEAD RD
OAK DR
BERWICK AVE
KIRKWALL RD
DINGWALL AVE
DAYTON CL
ELGIN CRES
SELKIRK PL
B3373
KINGSWAY GDNS
FORT TERR
CROWNHILL FORT RD
DUMFRIES AVE
B3413
COWLEY RD
MALORY CL
RUSKIN CRES
BRAKE RD
NICHOLSON RD
WHIN BANK RD
WHITLEIGH VILLAS
KIPLING GDNS
COPPICE GDNS
WHITLEIGH AVE
HAROLDSLEIGH AVE
MEAVY AVE
SOUTH VIEW
GORSEY CL
BUDSHEAD WAY
TAVISTOCK RD
PLUMER RD
GROSVENOR RD
CHARLTON RD
RICHMOND RD
SMALLACK DR
THE JAMES
HUNTER CL
SMALLACK CL
LANSDOWNE RD
CHARLTON
Crownhill
4
FROBISHER APP
WARSPITE GDNS
LEANDER WAY
MEAVY WAY
MORSHEAD RD
ALEXANDRA RD
TAILYOUR RD
CROWNHILL CT
WHITLEIGH COTTS
TEMERAIRE RD
BLADDER LA
COLERIDGE AVE
FORT AUSTIN AVE
B3413
RAMSEY GDNS
ABERDEEN AVE
CAPTAINS GDNS
JELLICOE RD
CROSS PARK RD
CROSS PARK AVE
CROSS PARK WAY
Liby
TREWITHY DR
TREWITHY CT
WIDEY CT
WIDEY CROSS
COSDON PL
RC Coll
CONQUEROR DR
GUARD CL
THE LAWNS
MANADON HILL
GREAT BERRY RD
BERRY HEAD GDNS
STANBURY AVE
MORETON AVE
ST JOSEPH CL
OAKTREE CT
WIDEY LA
BOWDEN PARK RD
WHITBY CRES
WINSBURY CT
3
PL5
SHACKLETON CT
BARRIE GDNS
Manadon
MANADON CL
Widey Court Prim Sch
PL6
Courtlands Sch
GRAINGE RD
20
LINKETTY LA
BELLAMY CL
58
BRONTE PL
PEPYS PL
MARRYAT GDNS
MANADON DR
TAVISTOCK RD
SOUTHWELL RD
ST BRIDGET AVE
HARDY CRES
ST PETERS RD
Sch
LINKETTY LA W
RUTHVEN CL
HOPTON CL
DITTON CT
COOBAN CT
CHARFIELD DR
HINGSTON CT
ST KEVERNE PL
TREVONE GDNS
MYLOR CL
DOWNGATE GDNS
ST PANCRAS AVE
DRAX GDNS
BURNETT RD
THE PARKWAY
WARDLOW GDNS
TREVANNION CL
CULVER CL
2
Liby
BROMHEAD CT
PARNELL CL
LEIGH CT
Hartley
PL2
TREVENEAGUE GDNS
ROSPEATH CRES
Manadon Wood
A386
B3250
LEIGHTON RD
KNEELE GDNS
ALLEYN GDNS
MAITLAND DR
MARGARET PK
BEAUMARIS GDNS
PENDENNIS CL
WARDLOW CL
WESTCOTT CL
ST ERTH RD
TRELOWETH CL
TREVESSA CL
CARNOCK RD
HARNORLEN RD
CORPORATION RD
CAMILLA TERR
TORLAND RD
CORFE AVE
POWDERHAM RD
BEAUMARIS RD
SARUM CL
A38
CULVER
Superstore
TOR RD
GLENTOR RD
TOR CRES
BROUGHTON CL
LOCKINGTON AVE
BEAUMARIS RD
HARLECH CL
BRECON CL
1
CHESTNUT RD
LIMETREE RD
EFFINGHAM CRES
TOR CL
GLENBURN CL
LYNDRICK RD
THE DRIVE
RUSSELL AVE
PL3
DYNEVOR CL
PEARN RIDGE
ST MARTIN'S AVE
POUNDS PARK RD
BURLEIGH MANOR
TORR LA
Hartley
BAINBRIDGE AVE
RICHARDS ROW
HILL LA
BRIAR RD
PEARN GDNS
PEARN RD
EASTFIELD
TORR VIEW AVE
BICKHAM PARK RD
BURLEIGH LA
BERROW PARK RD
BREAN DOWN RD
VENN WAY
VENN GDNS
CONSORT CL
HIGHER COMPTON RD
WIDEY VIEW
57
Sch
Higher Compton
BURLEIGH PARK RD
BURNHAM PARK RD
WEMBURY PARK RD
BREAN DOWN CL
VENN GR
VENN CRES
EDENSIDE
MANNAMEAD RD
RESERVOIR RD
HIGHER COMPTON RD
Sch
KINGSWOOD PARK AVE
WESTON PARK RD
HILLSDUNNE RD
VENN CT
HARTLEY RD
KINGSLAND GARDENS CL
HARTLEY CT
A
ENDSLEIGH PARK RD
48
CHURCHILL WAY
B
27
C
HARTLEY PARK GDNS
49
COMPTON LEIGH
FORTESCUE PL
THORNBURY PARK AVE
LEAT WLK
BEECHFIELD GR
THORNHILL WAY
VAPRON RD
EGGBUCKLAND RD
HARTLEY AVE
EDGCUMBE PARK RD
ROWDEN
THORNHILL RD
LOVELL RD
NEAGLE RD
HARTLEY AVE
WELLSBOURNE
COMPTON
PO
Liby

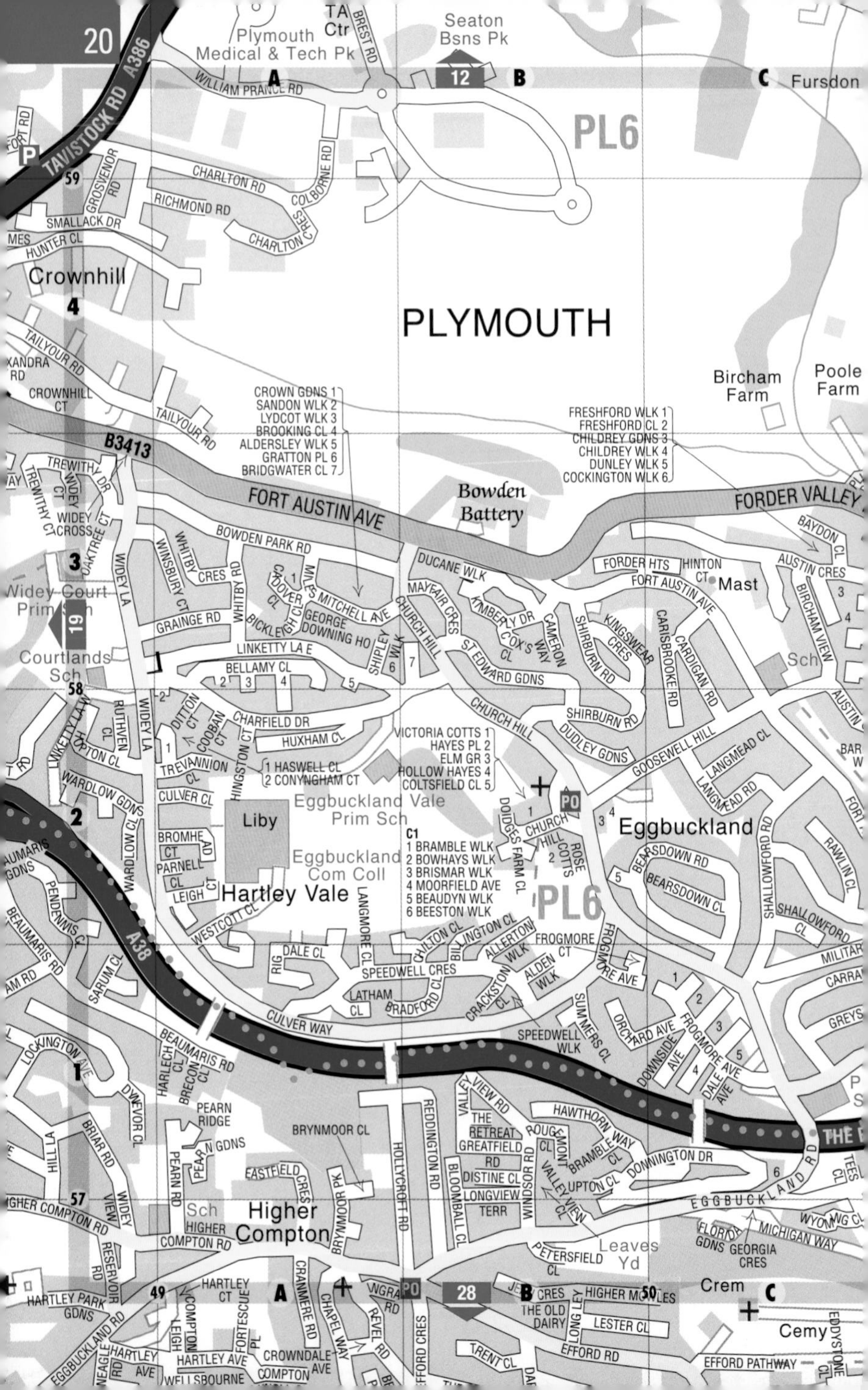

TA Ctr
BREST RD
Plymouth Medical & Tech Pk
Seaton Bsns Pk
12
A
B
C
Fursdon
A386
TAVISTOCK RD
WILLIAM PRANCE RD
PL6
COLBORNE RD
CHARLTON RD
RICHMOND RD
CHARLTON CRES
GROSVENOR RD
SMALLACK DR
HUNTER CL
59
Crownhill
4
PLYMOUTH
TAILYOUR RD
CROWNHILL CT
Bircham Farm
Poole Farm
CROWN GDNS 1
SANDON WLK 2
LYDCOT WLK 3
BROOKING CL 4
ALDERSLEY WLK 5
GRATTON PL 6
BRIDGWATER CL 7
FRESHFORD WLK 1
FRESHFORD CL 2
CHILDREY GDNS 3
CHILDREY WLK 4
DUNLEY WLK 5
COCKINGTON WLK 6
B3413
TREWITHY DR
TREWITHY CT
WIDEY CT
WIDEY CROSS
OAKTREE CT
FORT AUSTIN AVE
Bowden Battery
FORDER VALLEY
BAYDON CL
3
Widey Court Prim Sch
19
Courtlands Sch
WIDEY LA
WINSBURY CT
WHITBY CRES
BOWDEN PARK RD
WHITBY RD
GRAINGE RD
CADOVER CL
MILES MITCHELL AVE
BICKLEIGH CL
GEORGE DOWNING HO
LINKETTY LA E
BELLAMY CL
SHIPLEY WLK
CHURCH HILL
DUCANE WLK
MAYFAIR CRES
KIMBERLY DR
COX'S CL
CAMERON WAY
ST EDWARD GDNS
SHIRBURN RD
KINGSWEAR CRES
FORDER HTS
HINTON CT
Mast
FORT AUSTIN AVE
CARISBROOKE RD
CARDIGAN RD
AUSTIN CRES
BIRCHAM VIEW
Sch
58
LINKETTY LA W
HOPTON CL
RUTHVEN CL
DITTON CT
COOBAN CT
CHARFIELD DR
HUXHAM CL
HINGSTON CT
TREVANNION CL
1 HASWELL CL
2 CONYNGHAM CT
VICTORIA COTTS 1
HAYES PL 2
ELM GR 3
HOLLOW HAYES 4
COLTSFIELD CL 5
DUDLEY GDNS
GOOSEWELL HILL
LANGMEAD CL
LANGMEAD RD
WARDLOW GDNS
CULVER CL
Liby
Eggbuckland Vale Prim Sch
PO
Eggbuckland
2
BROMHEAD CT
PARNELL CL
LEIGH CT
Hartley Vale
Eggbuckland Com Coll
C1
1 BRAMBLE WLK
2 BOWHAYS WLK
3 BRISMAR WLK
4 MOORFIELD AVE
5 BEAUDYN WLK
6 BEESTON WLK
DOIDGES FARM CL
CHURCH HILL COTTS
ROSE COTTS
BEARSDOWN RD
BEARSDOWN CL
SHALLOWFORD RD
SHALLOWFORD CL
RAWLIN CL
PL6
BEAUMARIS GDNS
PENDENNIS CL
BEAUMARIS RD
WARDLOW CL
WESTCOTT CL
A38
RIGDALE CL
LANGMORE CL
CHILTON CL
BILLINGTON CL
ALLERTON WLK
FROGMORE CT
FROGMORE AVE
SPEEDWELL CRES
ALDEN WLK
CRACKSTON CL
LATHAM CL
BRADFORD CL
SARUM CL
CULVER WAY
SUMMERS CL
ORCHARD AVE
DOWNSIDE AVE
FROGMORE AVE
DALE AVE
SPEEDWELL WLK
LOCKINGTON AVE
1
HARLECH CL
BRECON CL
BEAUMARIS RD
DYNEVOR CL
PEARN RIDGE
BRYNMOOR CL
VALLEY VIEW RD
REDDINGTON RD
HAWTHORN WAY
THE RETREAT
GREATFIELD RD
ROUGEMONT CL
BRAMBLE CL
DONNINGTON DR
HILL LA
BRIAR RD
PEARN GDNS
PEARN RD
EASTFIELD CRES
DISTINE CL
LONGVIEW TERR
BLOOMBALL CL
WINDSOR RD
VALLEY VIEW CL
UPTON CL
EGGBUCKLAND RD
57
HIGHER COMPTON RD
WIDEY VIEW
Sch
HIGHER COMPTON RD
Higher Compton
BRYNMOOR PK
HOLLYCROFT RD
Leaves Yd
FLORIDA GDNS
GEORGIA CRES
MICHIGAN WAY
PETERSFIELD CL
RESERVOIR RD
HARTLEY PARK GDNS
49
HARTLEY CT
CRANMERE RD
A
PO
28
B
HIGHER MOULES
50
Crem
C
THE OLD DAIRY
LONG LEY
LESTER CL
Cemy
EGGBUCKLAND RD
LEIGH
COMPTON
FORTESCUE PL
CHAPEL WAY
REVEL RD
EFFORD CRES
HARTLEY AVE
CROWNDALE AVE
COMPTON AVE
WELLSBOURNE
TRENT CL
EFFORD RD
EFFORD PATHWAY
EDDYSTONE CL

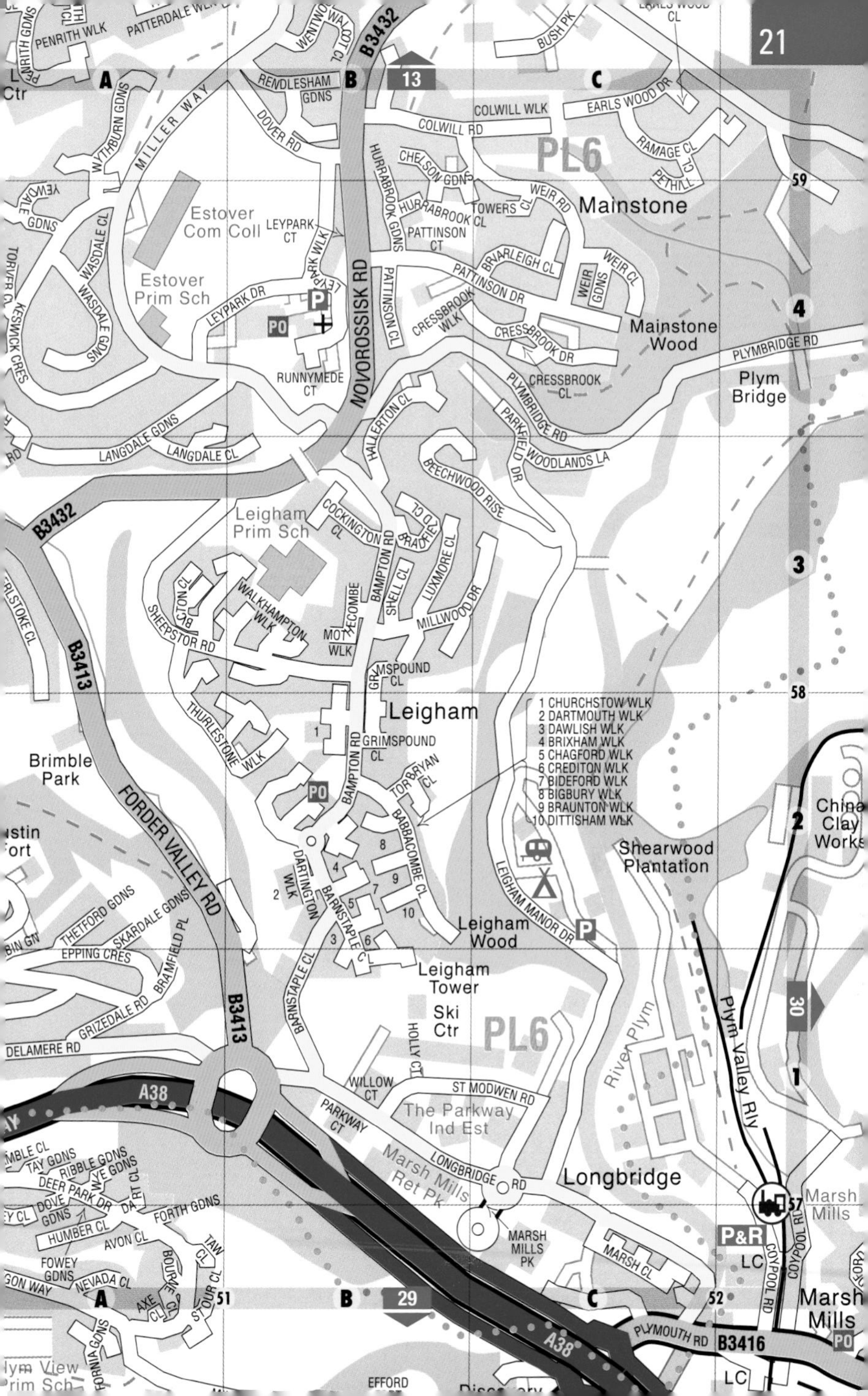

PENRITH GDNS
PATTERDALE WLK
PENRITH GDNS
WENTWORTH
WALCOT CL
B3432
BUSH PK
EARLS WOOD CL
13
RENDLESHAM GDNS
COLWILL WLK
EARLS WOOD DR
MILLER WAY
WYTHBURN GDNS
DOVER RD
COLWILL RD
RAMAGE CL
PL6
PETHILL CL
YEWDALE GDNS
CHELSON GDNS
HURRABROOK GDNS
HURRABROOK CL
TOWERS CL
WEIR RD
Mainstone
Estover Com Coll
LEYPARK CT
PATTINSON CT
WASDALE CL
TORVER CL
Estover Prim Sch
LEYPARK WLK
BRIARLEIGH CL
WEIR GDNS
WEIR CL
PATTINSON DR
LEYPARK DR
PATTINSON CL
CRESSBROOK WLK
Mainstone Wood
KESWICK CRES
WASDALE GDNS
PO
CRESSBROOK DR
PLYMBRIDGE RD
NOVOROSSISK RD
CRESSBROOK CL
Plym Bridge
RUNNYMEDE CT
HALLERTON CL
PLYMBRIDGE RD
PARKFIELD DR
LANGDALE GDNS
LANGDALE CL
WOODLANDS LA
BEECHWOOD RISE
B3432
Leigham Prim Sch
COCKINGTON CL
BRADFIELD CL
BAMPTON RD
LUXMORE CL
BUCKTON CL
WALKHAMPTON WLK
SHELL CL
LETCOMBE
MILLWOOD DR
SHEPSTOR RD
MOT WLK
GRIMSPOUND CL
B3413
Leigham
1 CHURCHSTOW WLK
2 DARTMOUTH WLK
3 DAWLISH WLK
4 BRIXHAM WLK
5 CHAGFORD WLK
6 CREDITON WLK
7 BIDEFORD WLK
8 BIGBURY WLK
9 BRAUNTON WLK
10 DITTISHAM WLK
THURLESTONE WLK
GRIMSPOUND CL
Brimble Park
TOR BRYAN CL
BAMPTON RD
BABBACOMBE CL
China Clay Works
Shearwood Plantation
FORDER VALLEY RD
DARTINGTON WLK
LEIGHAM MANOR DR
BARNSTAPLE CL
Leigham Wood
THETFORD GDNS
SKARDALE GDNS
BRAMFIELD PL
EPPING CRES
Leigham Tower
Ski Ctr
Plym Valley Rly
30
GRIZEDALE RD
PL6
River Plym
DELAMERE RD
HOLLY CT
B3413
A38
WILLOW CT
ST MODWEN RD
The Parkway Ind Est
PARKWAY CT
Marsh Mills Ret Pk
LONGBRIDGE RD
Longbridge
TAY GDNS
RIBBLE GDNS
WYE GDNS
DEER PARK DR
DART CL
DOVE GDNS
FORTH GDNS
HUMBER CL
AVON CL
TAW CL
MARSH MILLS PK
Marsh Mills
P&R
LC
FOWEY GDNS
NEVADA CL
BOURNE CL
MARSH CL
COYPOOL RD
AXE CL
STOUR CL
29
A38
PLYMOUTH RD
B3416
Marsh Mills
FORNIA GDNS
EFFORD
LC

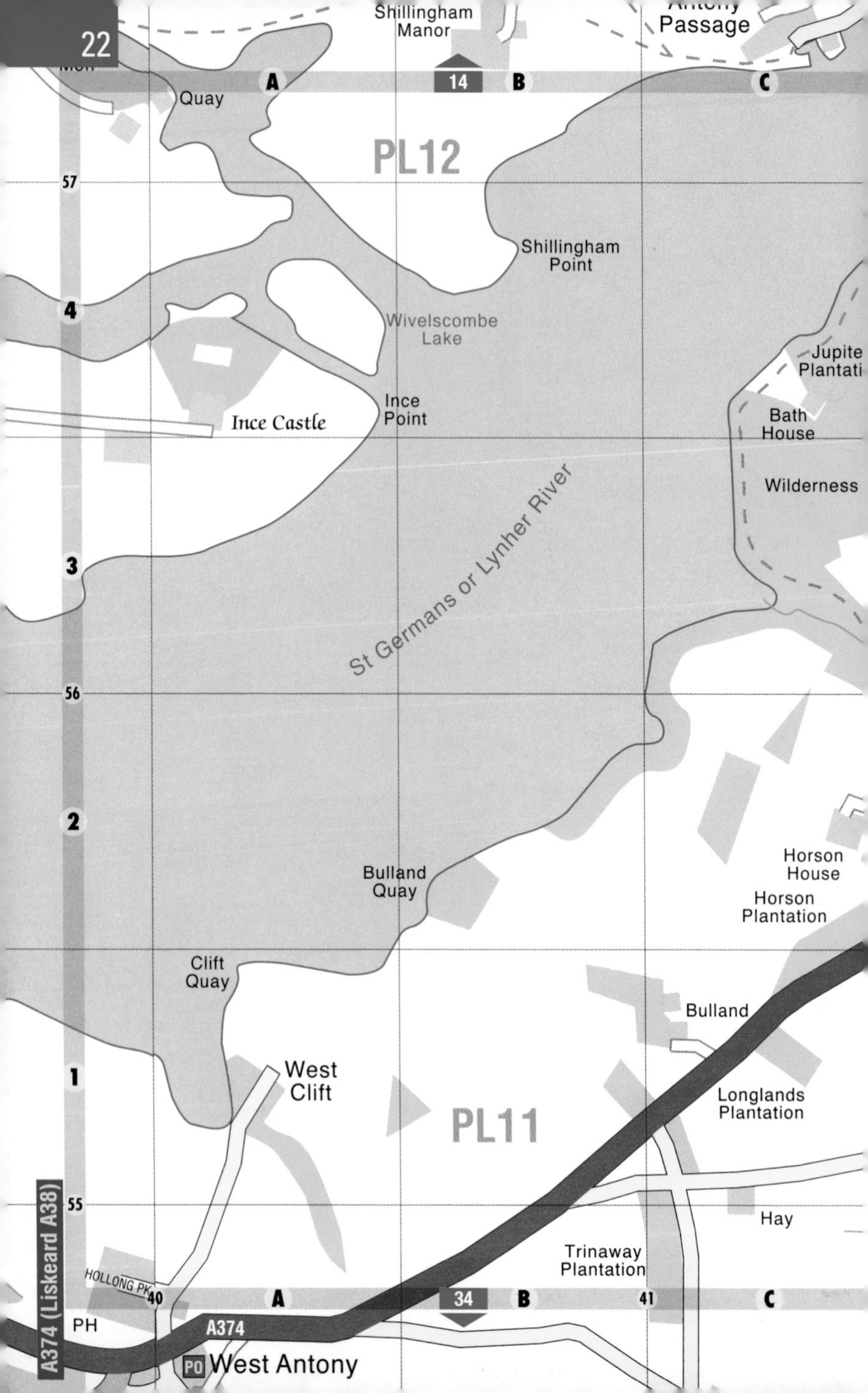
Shillingham
Manor
Antony
Passage
14
A
B
C
Quay
PL12
57
Shillingham
Point
4
Wivelscombe
Lake
Jupite
Plantati
Ince
Point
Ince Castle
Bath
House
Wilderness
St Germans or Lynher River
3
56
2
Bulland
Quay
Horson
House
Horson
Plantation
Clift
Quay
Bulland
1
West
Clift
Longlands
Plantation
PL11
55
Hay
Trinaway
Plantation
A374 (Liskeard A38)
HOLLONG PK
40
A
34
B
41
C
PH
A374
PO
West Antony

A
B
15
C
Beggar's Island
57
Higher Wearlands Plantation
Jetty
PL11
Great Kithill Plantation
North Wilcove
Antony Woodland Garden
Tomboy Hill
Wilcove
COVE MDW
PENGELLY PK
PH
Cangapool
Antony House
Antony Park
FERRY LA
WILCOVE LA
PENGELLY CL
PENGELLY HILL
Maryfield
Coombe Pk
24
56
Sports Gd
Borough Farm House
THE MEADOWS
1 FISTRAL CL
2 GWITHIAN CL
BOROUGH CT
PRIMROSE CL
KYNANCE CL
MULLION CL
BOROUGH PK
Mast
PENLEE PK
TREMATON CL
INCE CL
TREVITHICK AVE
SENNEN CL
Torpoint Com Sch
A374
LAMORNA PK
CARLYON CL
LANGDON DOWN WAY
CLEGG AVE
PENDENNIS CL
WOODLAND WAY
GROVE PK
KERNOW CL
WESTLAKE CL
PENTIRE RD
KERNOW CT 3
TRELAWNEY WAY 4
GOAD AVE
ADAMS CRES
Carbeile Jnr Sch
EVENDEN CT
TREVOL RD
Trevol Bsns Pk
FISGARD WAY
WAVISH PK
TRELAWNEY
GURNEY CL
FROBISHER WAY
HMS Fisgard
ADAMS CL
MURDOCK RD
DAVY CL
KHYBER CL
TRELAWNEY RISE
GOAD CL
SYCAMORE DR
PL11
Trevol Ho
TRENGROUSE AVE
HAWTHORN AVE
CHESTNUT CL
MAPLE AVE
BEECH CL
COLWYN RD
TREVOL RD
TREVOL PL
PENCAIR AVE
CEDAR CL
CEDAR DR
TREGONING RD
55
MILL LA
MILLHOUSE PK
TREVORDER RD
TREVORDER CL
PENDILLY AVE
42
35
43
HMS Raleigh

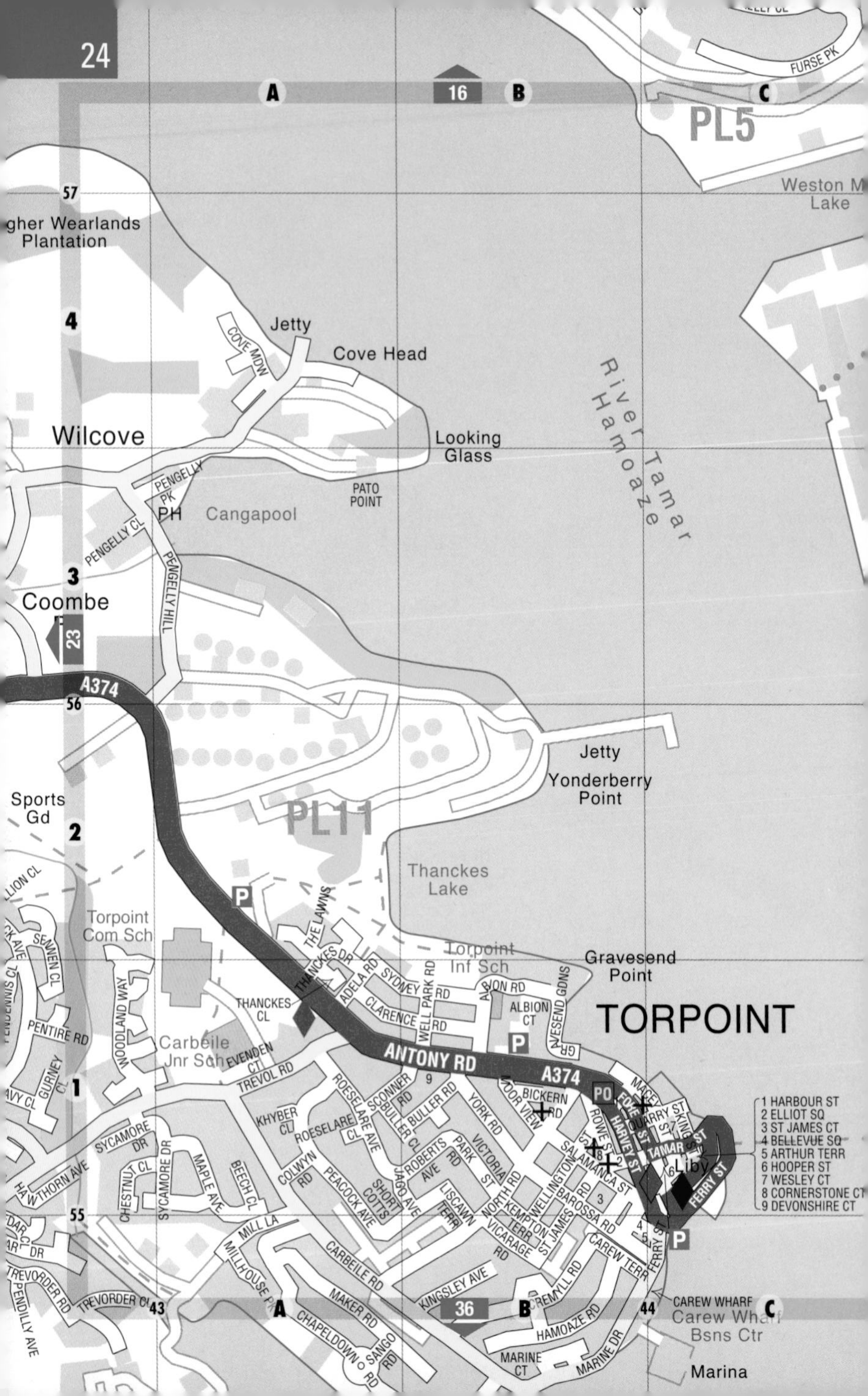

A
16
B
C
FURSE PK
PL5
Weston Mill Lake
57
gher Wearlands Plantation
4
Jetty
COVE MDW
Cove Head
River Tamar
Hamoaze
Wilcove
Looking Glass
PENGELLY PK
PATO POINT
PH
Cangapool
PENGELLY CL
PENGELLY HILL
3
Coombe
23
A374
56
Jetty
Yonderberry Point
Sports Gd
2
PL11
Thanckes Lake
P
THE LAWNS
Torpoint Com Sch
Torpoint Inf Sch
Gravesend Point
SENNEN CL
THANCKES DR
ADELA RD
SYDNEY RD
WELL PARK RD
ALBION RD
GRAVESEND GDNS
WOODLAND WAY
THANCKES CL
CLARENCE RD
ALBION CT
TORPOINT
PENTIRE RD
Carbeile Jnr Sch
EVENDEN CT
ANTONY RD
A374
GURNEY CL
1
TREVOL RD
9
BICKERN RD
MOOR VIEW
PO
FORE ST
MACEY ST
QUARRY ST
KING ST
HARVEY ST
ROWE ST
TAMAR ST
FERRY ST
Liby
KHYBER CL
ROESELARE CL
ROESELARE AVE
SCONNER RD
BULLER CL
BULLER RD
YORK RD
VICTORIA ST
SALAMANCA ST
WELLINGTON ST
SYCAMORE DR
CHESTNUT CL
SYCAMORE DR
MAPLE AVE
BEECH CL
HAWTHORN AVE
COLWYN RD
PEACOCK AVE
SHORT COTTS
JAGO AVE
ROBERTS AVE
PARK RD
LISCAWN TERR
NORTH RD
KEMPTON TERR
BAROSSA RD
ST JAMES RD
VICARAGE RD
CAREW TERR
1 HARBOUR ST
2 ELLIOT SQ
3 ST JAMES CT
4 BELLEVUE SQ
5 ARTHUR TERR
6 HOOPER ST
7 WESLEY CT
8 CORNERSTONE CT
9 DEVONSHIRE CT
55
MILL LA
MILLHOUSE PK
CARBEILE RD
KINGSLEY AVE
CREMYLL RD
TREVORDER RD
TREVORDER CL
PENDILLY AVE
43
A
MAKER RD
CHAPELDOWN RD
SANGO RD
36
B
HAMOAZE RD
44
CAREW WHARF
C
Carew Wharf Bsns Ctr
MARINE CT
MARINE DR
Marina

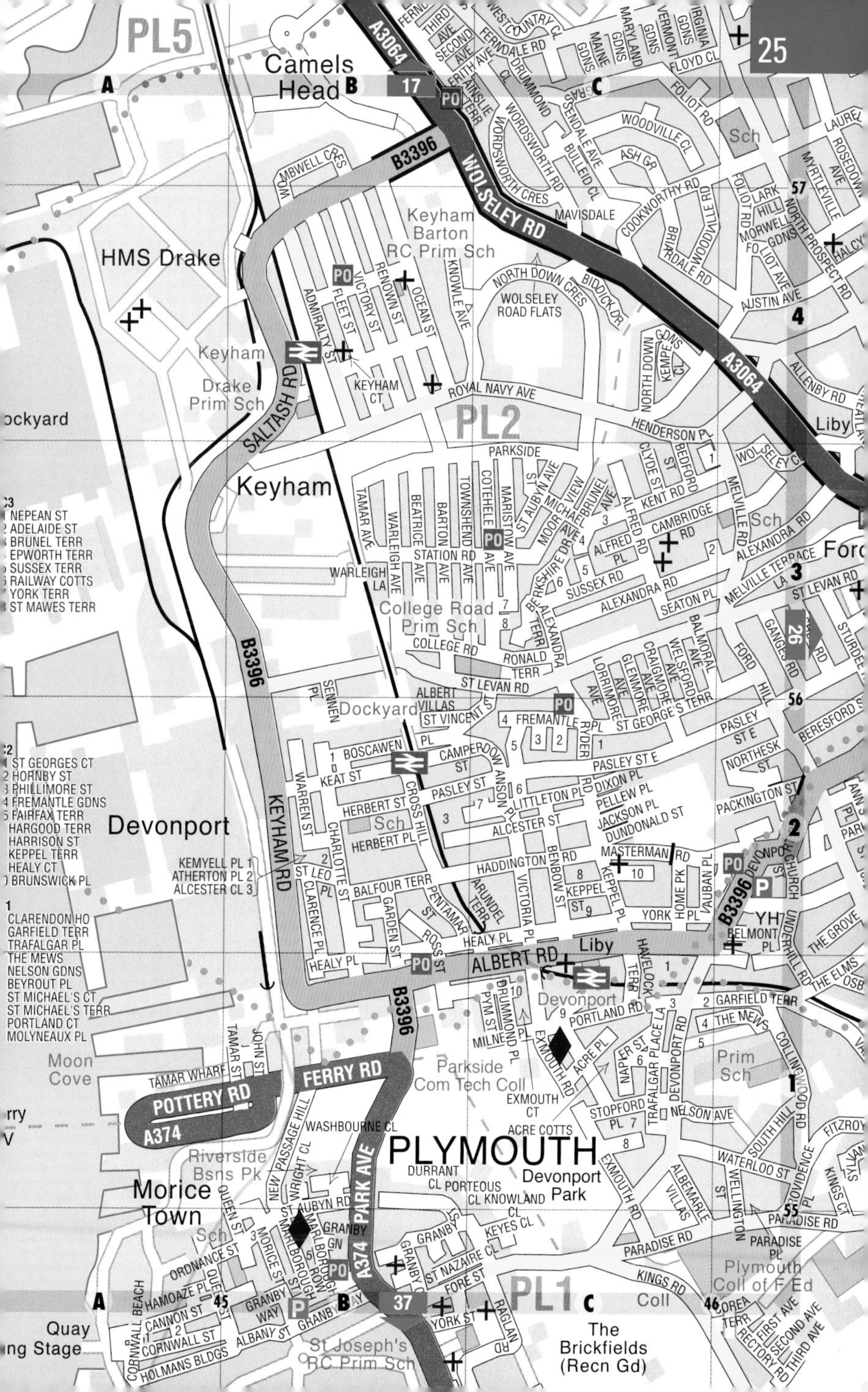
PL5
Camels Head
A
B
C
17
A3064
WOLSELEY RD
B3396
HMS Drake
Keyham
Drake Prim Sch
Keyham Barton RC Prim Sch
WOLSELEY ROAD FLATS
NORTH DOWN CRES
ROYAL NAVY AVE
PL2
SALTASH RD
Keyham
Dockyard
College Road Prim Sch
Dockyard
Devonport
KEYHAM RD
ALBERT RD
Liby
Devonport
Moon Cove
FERRY RD
POTTERY RD
A374
Riverside Bsns Pk
Morice Town
PLYMOUTH
Devonport Park
Parkside Com Tech Coll
PARK AVE
PL1
Plymouth Coll of F Ed
The Brickfields (Recn Gd)
St Joseph's RC Prim Sch
Quay
37
45
46
55
56
57
Ford
26
C3
NEPEAN ST
ADELAIDE ST
BRUNEL TERR
EPWORTH TERR
SUSSEX TERR
RAILWAY COTTS
YORK TERR
ST MAWES TERR
C2
ST GEORGES CT
HORNBY ST
PHILLIMORE ST
FREMANTLE GDNS
FAIRFAX TERR
HARGOOD TERR
HARRISON ST
KEPPEL TERR
HEALY CT
BRUNSWICK PL
CLARENDON HO
GARFIELD TERR
TRAFALGAR PL
THE MEWS
NELSON GDNS
BEYROUT PL
ST MICHAEL'S CT
ST MICHAEL'S TERR
PORTLAND CT
MOLYNEAUX PL
KEMYELL PL 1
ATHERTON PL 2
ALCESTER CL 3

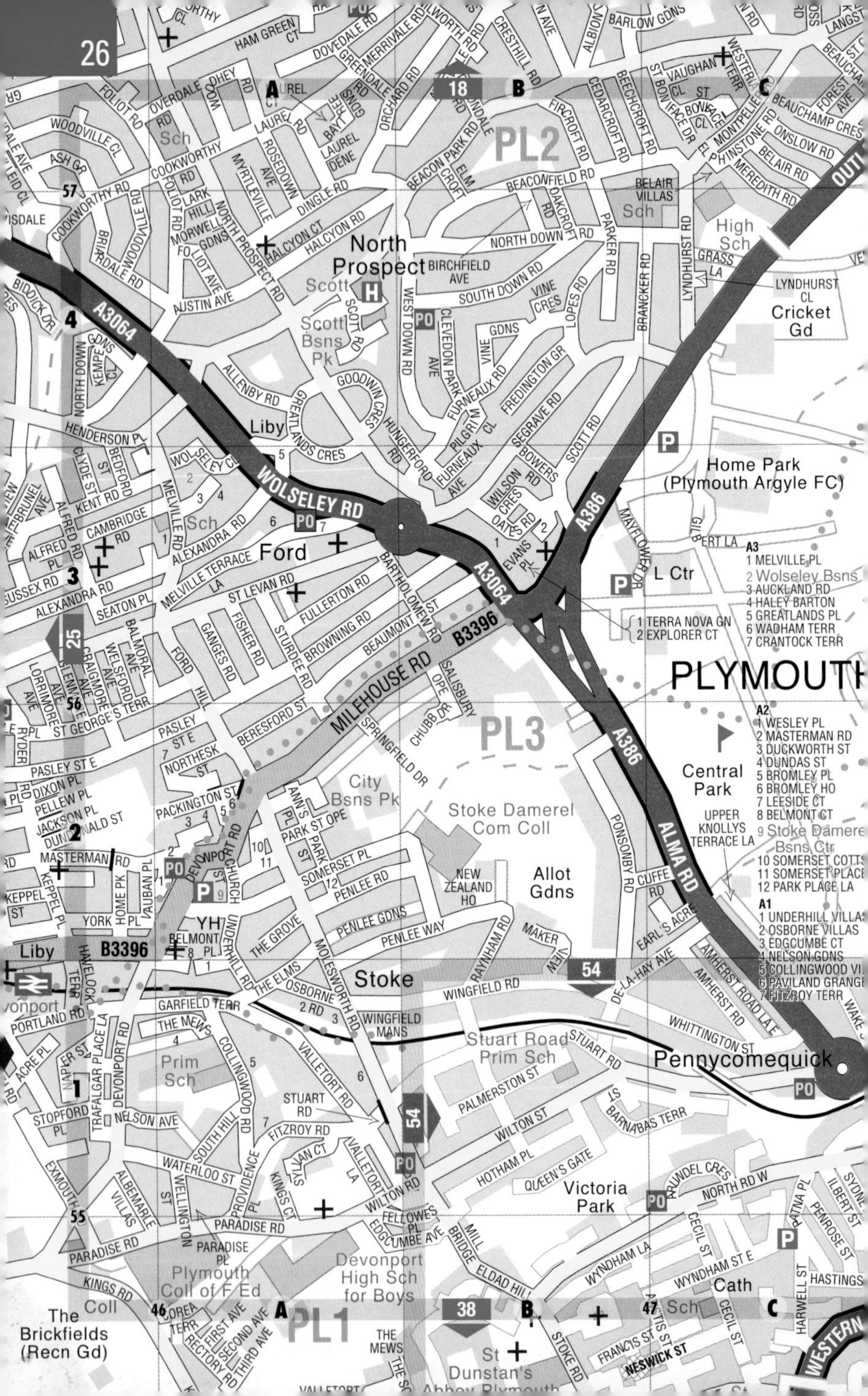

18
A
B
C
PL2
North Prospect
Scott
H
Scott Bsns Pk
PO
Liby
Ford
Sch
WOLSELEY RD
A3064
A386
B3396
MILEHOUSE RD
PL3
City Bsns Pk
Stoke Damerel Com Coll
Allot Gdns
NEW ZEALAND HO
Home Park (Plymouth Argyle FC)
L Ctr
Cricket Gd
High Sch
Belair Villas Sch
PLYMOUTH
Central Park
ALMA RD
Stoke
YH
Stuart Road Prim Sch
Pennycomequick
Victoria Park
Prim Sch
Plymouth Coll of F Ed
Devonport High Sch for Boys
The Brickfields (Recn Gd)
Coll
Cath
St Dunstan's Abbey Plymouth
PL1
25
54
38
57
56
55
46
47
1
2
3
4
A3
1 MELVILLE PL
2 Wolseley Bsns
3 AUCKLAND RD
4 HALEY BARTON
5 GREATLANDS PL
6 WADHAM TERR
7 CRANTOCK TERR
1 TERRA NOVA GN
2 EXPLORER CT
A2
1 WESLEY PL
2 MASTERMAN RD
3 DUCKWORTH ST
4 DUNDAS ST
5 BROMLEY PL
6 BROMLEY HO
7 LEESIDE CT
8 BELMONT CT
9 Stoke Damerel Bsns Ctr
10 SOMERSET COTTS
11 SOMERSET PLACE
12 PARK PLACE LA
A1
1 UNDERHILL VILLAS
2 OSBORNE VILLAS
3 EDGCUMBE CT
4 NELSON GDNS
5 COLLINGWOOD VI
6 PAVILAND GRANGE
7 FITZROY TERR
HAM GREEN CT
DOVEDALE RD
MERRIVALE RD
GREENDALE RD
ORCHARD RD
CRESTHILL RD
BARLOW GDNS
ALBION
VAUGHAN
WESTERN TERR
ST BONIFACE DR
BONIFACE CL
MONTPELIER RD
BEAUCHAMP CRES
FOREST AVE
ONSLOW RD
BELAIR RD
MEREDITH RD
ELPHINSTONE RD
FIRCROFT RD
CEDARCROFT RD
BEECHCROFT RD
BEACONFIELD RD
OAKCROFT RD
PARKER RD
LYNDHURST RD
LYNDHURST CL
GRASS LA
BRANCKER RD
NORTH DOWN RD
SOUTH DOWN RD
BIRCHFIELD AVE
VINE CRES
VINE GDNS
LOPES RD
BEACON PARK RD
ELM CROFT
FOLIOT RD
OVERDALE RD
LAUREL CT
LAUREL RD
LAUREL DENE
BAYTREE GDNS
ROSEDOWN AVE
MYRTLEVILLE RD
DINGLE RD
HALCYON RD
HALCYON CT
WOODVILLE CL
ASH GR
COOKWORTHY RD
LARK HILL
MORWELL GDNS
NORTH PROSPECT RD
FOLIOT AVE
AUSTIN AVE
BRIARDALE RD
WOODVILLE RD
BIDDICK DR
NORTH DOWN GDNS
KEMPE CL
SCOTT RD
WEST DOWN RD
CLEVEDON PARK AVE
FURNEAUX RD
FREDINGTON GR
SEGRAVE RD
SCOTT RD
BOWERS RD
PILGRIM CL
FURNEAUX AVE
GOODWIN CRES
HUNGERFORD RD
ALLENBY RD
GREATLANDS CRES
HENDERSON PL
WOLSELEY CL
MELVILLE RD
ALEXANDRA RD
CLYDE ST
BEDFORD ST
KENT RD
ALFRED RD
ALFRED PL
CAMBRIDGE RD
BRUNEL AVE
SUSSEX RD
SEATON PL
MELVILLE TERRACE LA
ST LEVAN RD
FULLERTON RD
BARTHOLOMEW RD
BROWNING RD
BEAUMONT ST
STURDEE RD
FISHER RD
GANGES RD
FORD HILL
BALMORAL AVE
WELSFORD AVE
CRAIGMORE AVE
GLENMORE AVE
LORRIMORE AVE
ST GEORGE'S TERR
RYDER
PASLEY ST E
PASLEY ST E
NORTHESK ST
BERESFORD ST
SPRINGFIELD DR
CHUBB DR
SALISBURY OPE
WILSON CRES
OATES RD
EVANS PL
MAYFLOWER DR
GILBERT LA
DIXON PL
PELLEW PL
JACKSON PL
DUNDONALD ST
PACKINGTON ST
MASTERMAN RD
KEPPEL PL
KEPPEL ST
HOME PK
VAUBAN PL
DEVONPORT RD
CHURCH ST
ANN'S PL
PARK ST OPE
PARK ST
SOMERSET PL
PENLEE RD
PENLEE GDNS
PENLEE WAY
THE GROVE
UNDERHILL RD
BELMONT PL
YORK PL
HAVELOCK TERR
MOLESWORTH RD
RAYNHAM RD
MAKER VIEW
PONSONBY RD
CUFFE RD
EARL'S ACRE
UPPER KNOLLYS TERRACE LA
AMHERST ROAD LA E
AMHERST RD
DE-LA-HAY AVE
WINGFIELD RD
WHITTINGTON ST
STUART RD
WAKE
THE ELMS
OSBORNE RD
WINGFIELD MANS
GARFIELD TERR
THE MEWS
PORTLAND RD
TRAFALGAR PLACE LA
DEVONPORT RD
NAPIER ST
ACRE PL
COLLINGWOOD RD
VALLETORT RD
STUART RD
PALMERSTON ST
BARNABAS TERR
STOPFORD PL
NELSON AVE
SOUTH HILL
FITZROY RD
WATERLOO ST
WELLINGTON ST
PROVIDENCE PL
KINGS CT
SYLVAN CT
VALLETORT LA
WILTON RD
WILTON ST
HOTHAM PL
QUEEN'S GATE
ARUNDEL CRES
NORTH RD W
PATNA PL
PENROSE ST
ILBERT ST
SYDNEY
EXMOUTH RD
ALBEMARLE VILLAS
PARADISE RD
PARADISE PL
FELLOWES PL
EDGCUMBE AVE
MILL BRIDGE
ELDAD HILL
WYNDHAM LA
WYNDHAM ST E
CECIL ST
HARWELL ST
HASTINGS
KINGS RD
COREA TERR
FIRST AVE
SECOND AVE
THIRD AVE
RECTORY RD
THE MEWS
STOKE RD
FRANCIS ST
NESWICK ST
WESTERN
Liby
Devonport

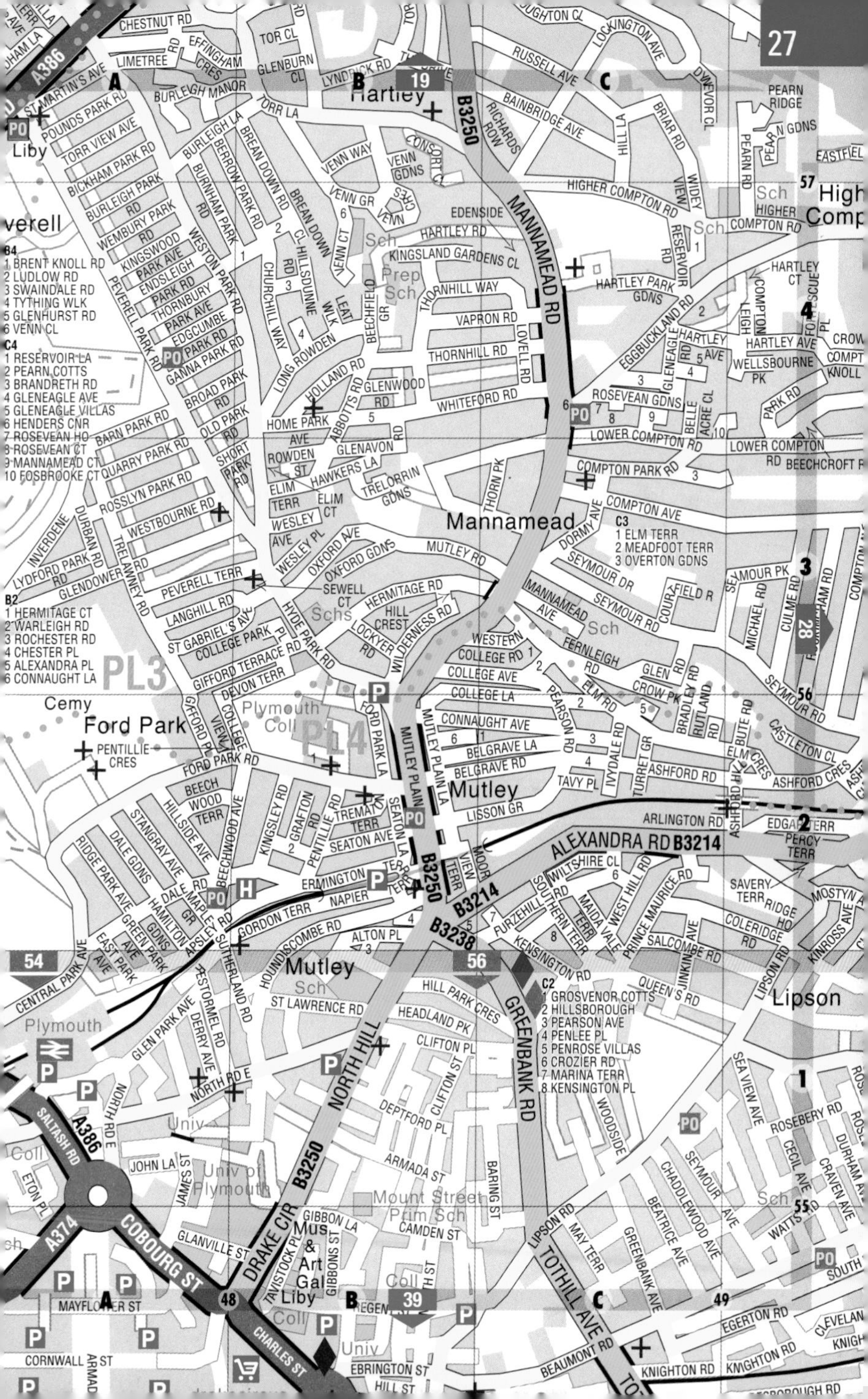
A
B
C
19
Hartley
B3250
Liby
Peverell
B4
1 BRENT KNOLL RD
2 LUDLOW RD
3 SWAINDALE RD
4 TYTHING WLK
5 GLENHURST RD
6 VENN CL
C4
1 RESERVOIR LA
2 PEARN COTTS
3 BRANDRETH RD
4 GLENEAGLE AVE
5 GLENEAGLE VILLAS
6 HENDERS CNR
7 ROSEVEAN HO
8 ROSEVEAN CT
9 MANNAMEAD CT
10 FOSBROOKE CT
B2
1 HERMITAGE CT
2 WARLEIGH RD
3 ROCHESTER RD
4 CHESTER PL
5 ALEXANDRA PL
6 CONNAUGHT LA
C3
1 ELM TERR
2 MEADFOOT TERR
3 OVERTON GDNS
C2
1 GROSVENOR COTTS
2 HILLSBOROUGH
3 PEARSON AVE
4 PENLEE PL
5 PENROSE VILLAS
6 CROZIER RD
7 MARINA TERR
8 KENSINGTON PL
CHESTNUT RD
LIMETREE RD
EFFINGHAM CRES
TOR CL
GLENBURN CL
LYNDRICK RD
BURLEIGH MANOR
ST MARTIN'S AVE
POUNDS PARK RD
TORR VIEW AVE
BICKHAM PARK RD
BURLEIGH PARK RD
WEMBURY PARK RD
KINGSWOOD PARK AVE
ENDSLEIGH PARK RD
THORNBURY PARK AVE
EDGCUMBE PARK RD
GANNA PARK RD
BROAD PARK RD
OLD PARK RD
SHORT PARK RD
BARN PARK RD
QUARRY PARK RD
ROSSLYN PARK RD
WESTBOURNE RD
PEVERELL PARK RD
WESTON PARK RD
BURLEIGH LA
BERROW PARK RD
BURNHAM PARK RD
BREAN DOWN RD
BREAN DOWN CL
HILLSDUNNE RD
CHURCHILL WAY
LEAT WLK
LONG ROWDEN
TORR LA
VENN WAY
VENN GDNS
CONSORT CL
VENN GR
VENN CRES
VENN CT
Sch
Prep Sch
BEECHFIELD GR
HOLLAND RD
ABBOTTS RD
GLENWOOD RD
HOME PARK AVE
ROWDEN ST
GLENAVON RD
HAWKERS LA
TRELORRIN GDNS
ELIM TERR
ELIM CT
WESLEY AVE
WESLEY PL
OXFORD AVE
OXFORD GDNS
MUTLEY RD
SEWELL CT
HERMITAGE RD
HILL CREST
WILDERNESS RD
LOCKYER RD
HYDE PARK RD
PEVERELL TERR
LANGHILL RD
ST GABRIEL'S AVE
COLLEGE PARK PL
GIFFORD TERRACE RD
DEVON TERR
Schs
INVERDENE
DURBAN RD
TRELAWNEY RD
LYDFORD PARK RD
GLENDOWER RD
PL3
PL4
Cemy
Ford Park
PENTILLIE CRES
GIFFORD PL
COLLEGE VIEW
Plymouth Coll
FORD PARK RD
FORD PARK LA
BEECH WOOD TERR
HILLSIDE AVE
BEECHWOOD AVE
STANGRAY AVE
DALE GDNS
RIDGE PARK AVE
KINGSLEY RD
GRAFTON RD
PENTILLIE RD
TREMATON TERR
SEATON AVE
SEATON LA
ERMINGTON TERR
NAPIER TERR
GORDON TERR
DALE RD
MAPLE GR
HAMILTON GDNS
GREEN PARK AVE
EAST PARK AVE
CENTRAL PARK AVE
APSLEY RD
SUTHERLAND RD
HOUNDISCOMBE RD
ALTON PL
Mutley
Mutley Plain
MUTLEY PLAIN LA
B3214
B3238
54
56
RUSSELL AVE
LOCKINGTON AVE
DYNEVOR CL
BAINBRIDGE AVE
RICHARDS ROW
HILL LA
BRIAR RD
PEARN RIDGE
PEARN RD
PEARN GDNS
EASTFIELD
HIGHER COMPTON RD
WIDEY VIEW
RESERVOIR RD
Higher Compton
57
MANNAMEAD RD
EDENSIDE
HARTLEY RD
KINGSLAND GARDENS CL
THORNHILL WAY
VAPRON RD
THORNHILL RD
LOVELL RD
WHITEFORD RD
HARTLEY PARK GDNS
HARTLEY CT
EGGBUCKLAND RD
GLENEAGLE RD
HARTLEY AVE
COMPTON LEIGH
FORTESCUE PL
CROWNHILL
COMPTON KNOLL
WELLSBOURNE PK
PARK RD
ROSEVEAN GDNS
BELLE ACRE CL
LOWER COMPTON RD
BEECHCROFT RD
COMPTON PARK RD
THORN PK
COMPTON AVE
Mannamead
DORMY AVE
SEYMOUR DR
SEYMOUR RD
COURTFIELD RD
SEYMOUR PK
MICHAEL RD
CULME RD
COMPTON
MANNAMEAD AVE
FERNLEIGH RD
GLEN RD
CROW PK
BRADLEY RD
RUTLAND RD
BUTE RD
CASTLETON CL
ELM CRES
ASHFORD CRES
ASHFORD RD
ASHFORD HILL
WESTERN COLLEGE RD
COLLEGE AVE
COLLEGE LA
CONNAUGHT AVE
BELGRAVE LA
BELGRAVE RD
PEARSON RD
ELM RD
IVYDALE RD
TURRET GR
TAVY PL
LISSON GR
MOOR VIEW TERR
ARLINGTON RD
ALEXANDRA RD
EDGAR TERR
PERCY TERR
WILTSHIRE CL
SOUTHERN TERR
FURZEHILL RD
MAIDA VALE TERR
WEST HILL RD
PRINCE MAURICE RD
SAVERY TERR
RIDGE HO
MOSTYN AVE
KINROSS AVE
COLERIDGE RD
SALCOMBE RD
JINKINS AVE
LIPSON RD
KENSINGTON RD
QUEEN'S RD
Lipson
28
Plymouth
SALTASH RD
A386
A374
COBOURG ST
CHARLES ST
48
39
49
55
Coll
ETON PL
JOHN LA
JAMES ST
Univ
Univ of Plymouth
NORTH RD E
GLEN PARK AVE
DERRY AVE
RESTORMEL RD
ST LAWRENCE RD
HEADLAND PK
HILL PARK CRES
GREENBANK RD
CLIFTON PL
CLIFTON ST
DEPTFORD PL
ARMADA ST
BARING ST
Mount Street Prim Sch
CAMDEN ST
GIBBON LA
GIBBONS ST
TAVISTOCK PL
DRAKE CIR
NORTH HILL
Mus & Art Gal
GLANVILLE ST
MAYFLOWER ST
CORNWALL ST
REGENT ST
EBRINGTON ST
HILL ST
WOODSIDE
CHADDLEWOOD AVE
SEYMOUR AVE
BEATRICE AVE
GREENBANK AVE
MAY TERR
TOTHILL AVE
BEAUMONT RD
KNIGHTON RD
EGERTON RD
CLEVELAND
SEA VIEW AVE
ROSEBERY RD
CECIL AVE
CRAVEN AVE
DURHAM AVE
WATTS RD
SOUTH

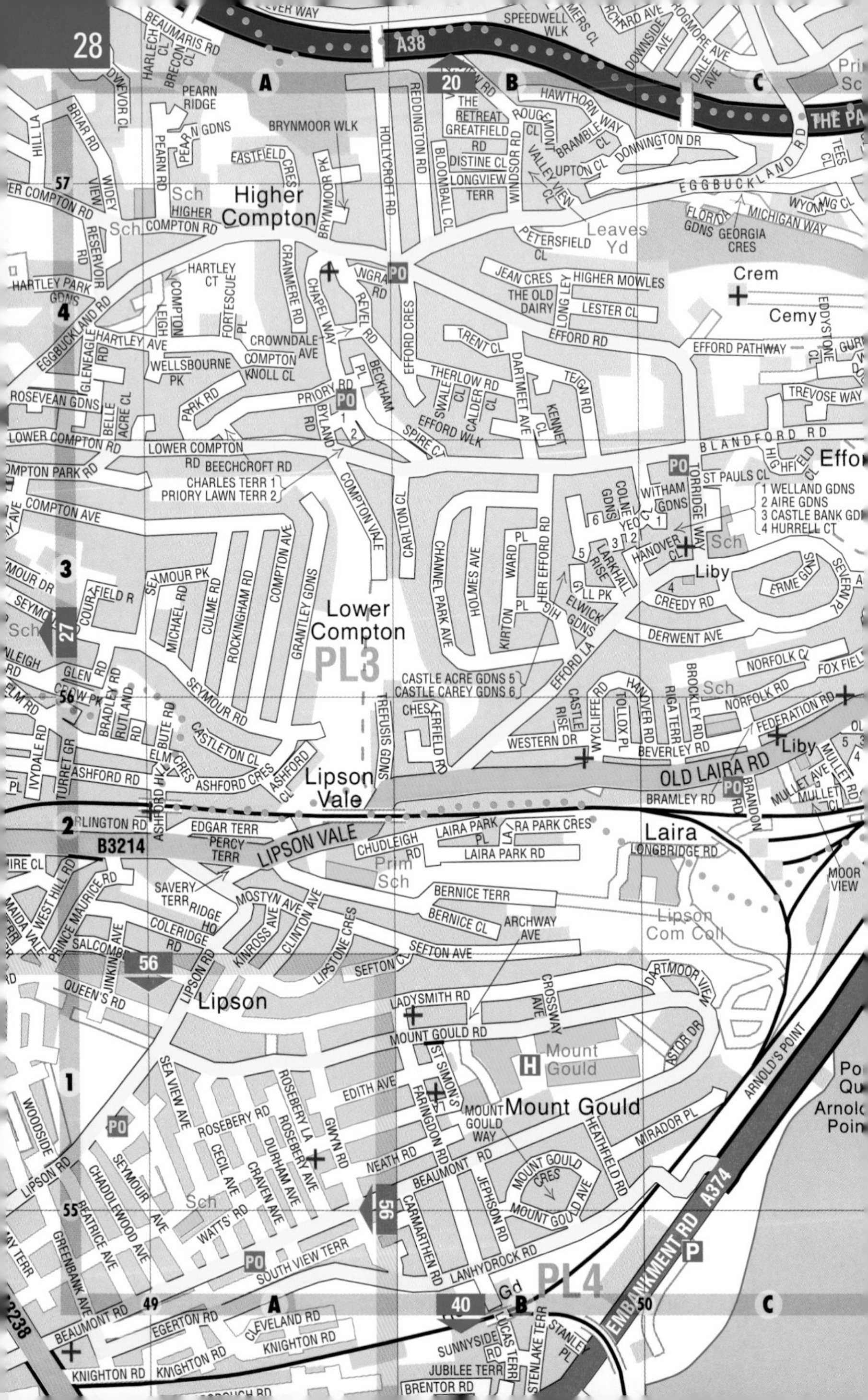
A38
20
A
B
C
SPEEDWELL WLK
BEAUMARIS RD
HARLECH CL
BRECON CL
DYNEVOR CL
PEARN RIDGE
PEARN GDNS
PEARN RD
BRYNMOOR WLK
EASTFIELD CRES
BRYNMOOR PK
HOLLYCROFT RD
REDDINGTON RD
THE RETREAT
GREATFIELD RD
DISTINE CL
LONGVIEW TERR
BLOOMBALL CL
WINDSOR RD
ROUGEMONT CL
VALLEY VIEW CL
HAWTHORN WAY
BRAMBLE CL
UPTON CL
DONNINGTON DR
DOWNSIDE AVE
HOGMORE AVE
DALE AVE
THE PA
EGGBUCKLAND RD
TEES CL
WYOMING CL
MICHIGAN WAY
FLORIDA GDNS
GEORGIA CRES
Leaves Yd
PETERSFIELD CL
HILL LA
BRIAR RD
WIDEY VIEW
57
COMPTON RD
Sch
Higher Compton
HIGHER COMPTON RD
RESERVOIR RD
HARTLEY PARK GDNS
HARTLEY CT
COMPTON LEIGH
FORTESCUE PL
CRANMERE RD
CHAPEL WAY
WGRAM RD
REVEL RD
PO
EFFORD CRES
JEAN CRES
HIGHER MOWLES
THE OLD DAIRY
LONG LEY
LESTER CL
Crem
Cemy
EDDYSTONE CL
4
EGGBUCKLAND RD
GLENEAGLE RD
HARTLEY AVE
WELLSBOURNE PK
CROWNDALE AVE
COMPTON KNOLL CL
TRENT CL
EFFORD RD
EFFORD PATHWAY
ROSEVEAN GDNS
BELLE ACRE CL
PARK RD
PRIORY RD
PL
BECKHAM
THERLOW RD
SWALE CL
CALDER CL
DARTMEET AVE
TEIGN RD
KENNET CL
TREVOSE WAY
BYLAND RD
EFFORD WLK
SPIRE CT
LOWER COMPTON RD
BEECHCROFT RD
BLANDFORD RD
COMPTON PARK RD
CHARLES TERR 1
PRIORY LAWN TERR 2
COMPTON VALE
CARLTON CL
PO
TORRIDGE WAY
ST PAULS CL
HIGHFIELD CL
Efford
COLNE GDNS
WITHAM GDNS
YEO CL
1 WELLAND GDNS
2 AIRE GDNS
3 CASTLE BANK GDNS
4 HURRELL CT
COMPTON AVE
CHANNEL PARK AVE
HOLMES AVE
WARD PL
KIRTON PL
HIGHER EFFORD RD
LARKHALL RISE
HANOVER CT
Sch
Liby
3
SEYMOUR DR
SEYMOUR PK
MICHAEL RD
CULME RD
ROCKINGHAM RD
COMPTON AVE
GRANTLEY GDNS
Lower Compton
PL3
GILL PK
ELWICK GDNS
CREEDY RD
ERME GDNS
SEVERN PL
COURTFIELD R
27
GLEN RD
BRADLEY RD
RUTLAND RD
SEYMOUR RD
CASTLETON CL
DERWENT AVE
EFFORD LA
CASTLE ACRE GDNS 5
CASTLE CAREY GDNS 6
NORFOLK CL
FOX FIELD
NORFOLK RD
FEDERATION RD
56
ELM RD
CROW PK
BUTE RD
ELM CRES
IVYDALE RD
TURRET GR
ASHFORD RD
ASHFORD HL
ASHFORD CRES
ASHFORD CL
TREFUSIS GDNS
CHESTERFIELD RD
CASTLE RISE
WYCLIFFE RD
TOLLOX PL
HANOVER RD
RIGA TERR
BROCKLEY RD
WESTERN DR
BEVERLEY RD
Liby
Lipson Vale
OLD LAIRA RD
PO
BRAMLEY RD
BRANDON RD
MULLET AVE
MULLET CL
2
ARLINGTON RD
EDGAR TERR
B3214
PERCY TERR
LIPSON VALE
CHUDLEIGH RD
LAIRA PARK PL
LAIRA PARK CRES
LAIRA PARK RD
Laira
LONGBRIDGE RD
MOOR VIEW
WEST HILL RD
PRINCE MAURICE RD
SAVERY TERR
RIDGE HO
MOSTYN AVE
CLINTON AVE
Prim Sch
BERNICE TERR
BERNICE CL
ARCHWAY AVE
Lipson Com Coll
MAIDA VALE
COLERIDGE RD
SALCOMBE
JINKINS AVE
KINROSS AVE
LIPSTONE CRES
SEFTON CL
SEFTON AVE
56
LIPSON RD
QUEEN'S RD
Lipson
LADYSMITH RD
CROSSWAY AVE
DARTMOOR VIEW
MOUNT GOULD RD
ST SIMON'S
Mount Gould
ASTOR DR
1
WOODSIDE
SEA VIEW AVE
EDITH AVE
FARINGDON RD
MOUNT GOULD WAY
Mount Gould
HEATHFIELD RD
MIRADOR PL
ARNOLD'S POINT
ROSEBERY RD
ROSEBERY LA
ROSEBERY AVE
GWYN RD
PO
SEYMOUR AVE
CECIL AVE
CRAVEN AVE
DURHAM AVE
NEATH RD
BEAUMONT RD
JEPHSON RD
MOUNT GOULD CRES
MOUNT GOULD AVE
A374
LIPSON RD
CHADDLEWOOD AVE
55
BEATRICE AVE
GREENBANK AVE
WATTS' RD
CARMARTHEN RD
EMBANKMENT RD
P
PO
SOUTH VIEW TERR
LANHYDROCK RD
PL4
49
40
50
Gd
BEAUMONT RD
EGERTON RD
CLEVELAND RD
KNIGHTON RD
SUNNYSIDE RD
LUCAS TERR
STENLAKE TERR
STANLEY PL
JUBILEE TERR
BRENTOR RD
Pom Qu
Arnold Point

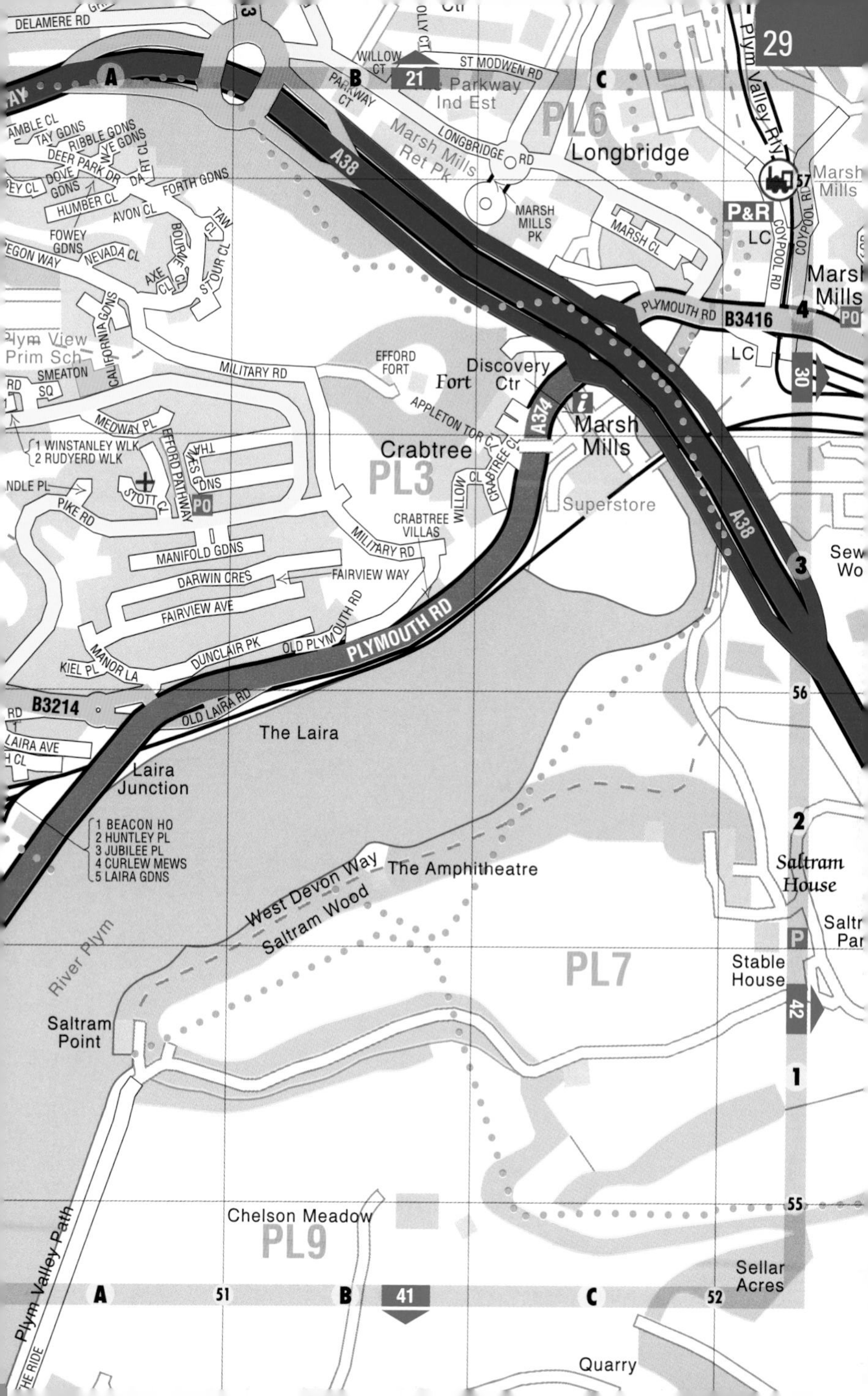
29
DELAMERE RD
WILLOW CT
ST MODWEN RD
PARKWAY CT
21
Parkway Ind Est
PL6
Longbridge
Plym Valley Rly
LONGBRIDGE RD
Marsh Mills Ret Pk
MARSH MILLS PK
MARSH CL
57
Marsh Mills
P&R
LC
COYPOOL RD
A38
AMBLE CL
TAY GDNS
RIBBLE GDNS
WYE GDNS
DEER PARK DR
DOVE GDNS
HUMBER CL
FORTH GDNS
AVON CL
TAW CL
FOWEY GDNS
NEVADA CL
EGON WAY
BOURNE CL
AXE CL
STOUR CL
CALIFORNIA GDNS
Plym View Prim Sch
SMEATON SQ
MILITARY RD
EFFORD FORT
Discovery Ctr
Fort
PLYMOUTH RD
B3416
4
PO
LC
30
APPLETON TOR CL
A374
Marsh Mills
MEDWAY PL
1 WINSTANLEY WLK
2 RUDYERD WLK
EFFORD PATHWAY
THAMES GDNS
Crabtree
PL3
WILLOW CL
CRABTREE CL
Superstore
STOTT CL
PO
PIKE RD
CRABTREE VILLAS
MILITARY RD
MANIFOLD GDNS
DARWIN CRES
FAIRVIEW WAY
FAIRVIEW AVE
OLD PLYMOUTH RD
PLYMOUTH RD
DUNCLAIR PK
MANOR LA
KIEL PL
3
Sew Wo
B3214
OLD LAIRA RD
LAIRA AVE
56
The Laira
Laira Junction
1 BEACON HO
2 HUNTLEY PL
3 JUBILEE PL
4 CURLEW MEWS
5 LAIRA GDNS
West Devon Way
The Amphitheatre
2
Saltram House
Saltram Wood
River Plym
P
PL7
Stable House
42
Saltram Point
1
55
Chelson Meadow
PL9
Plym Valley Path
Sellar Acres
A
51
B
41
C
52
Quarry
THE RIDE

A
B
C
PLYMBRIDGE RD
58
Triumphal Arch
China Clay Works
Hilltops
4
Shearwood Plantation
21
PL7
P
PL6
Plym Valley Rly
River Plym
3
ASHCOMBE CL
PLYMTREE DR
CRANFIELD
HIGHER WOODFORD LA
PLYMBRIDGE RD
CUNDY CL
TITHE RD
WHEATRIDGE
CHURCH CL
LONGACRE
GWEN DR
WOODFORD AVE
OAKAPPLE CL
ST MARGARETS RD
BRADDONS HILL
LITCHATON WAY
LITCHATON CRES
LITCHATON
Woodford
PLYMBRIDGE GDNS
PARK CL
GREENWAY AVE
Woodford Jun Sch
LARKHAM LA
FARM CL
REYNOLDS RD
Longbridge
57
Marsh Mills
COYPOOL RD
P&R
WOODFORD CL
WOODFORD CRES
WOODFORD GN
Sch
HARRIET GDNS
Hele's Sch
MARSH CL
LC
THE KNOLL
LYNWOOD AVE
GREAT WOODFORD DR
THE DELL
LARKHAM CL
ST MARY'S RD
WREN GDNS
SHEARWOOD CL
STONEBAR
2
B3416
PO
COPPARD MDWS
SEYMOUR RD
A38
UNICORN CL
MOLESWORTH RD
DINGLE RD
OAKFIELD RD
MORLEY VIEW RD
i
Cot Hill Trad Est
PLYMOUTH RD
Ret Pk
Trad Est
CHANTRY CT
MARSHALL RD
Ind & Trad Est
29
LINKETTY LA
VALLEY RD
Sewage Works
COT HILL
Underwood
1
DUDLEY RD
PL3
MAIDENWELL RD
BROOKINGFIELD
UNDERLANE
MORLEY CL
ROMILLY GDNS
MERAFIELD CL
MAPLE GR
ELAINE CL
ROBERT ADAMS CL
PARKER CL
SOVEREIGN CT
56
MERAFIELD RD
MERAFIELD RISE
GRANTHAM CL
WOODLAND DR
AMADOS CL
MERAFIELD DR
52
42
53
AMADOS RISE
AMADOS DR
MERAFIELD FARM COTTS
Amados Hill
Saltram House
Hardwick Wood

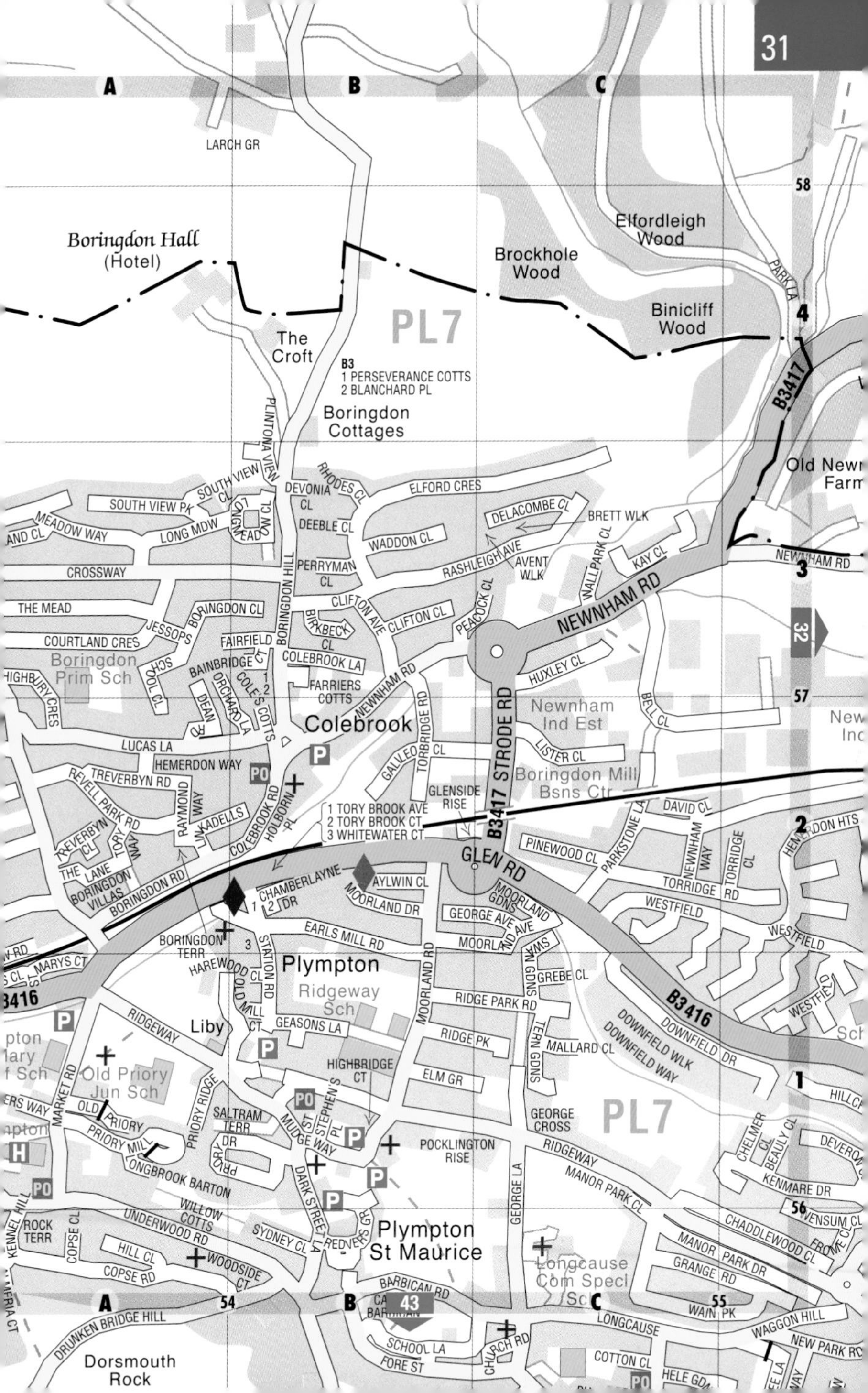

Boringdon Hall (Hotel)
The Croft
PL7
B3
1 PERSEVERANCE COTTS
2 BLANCHARD PL
Boringdon Cottages
Brockhole Wood
Elfordleigh Wood
Binicliff Wood
Old Newnham Farm
LARCH GR
PARK LA
B3417
NEWNHAM RD
ELFORD CRES
DELACOMBE CL
BRETT WLK
RASHLEIGH AVE
AVENT WLK
WALLPARK CL
KAY CL
WADDON CL
RHODES CL
DEVONIA CL
DEEBLE CL
PERRYMAN CL
SOUTH VIEW CL
SOUTH VIEW PK
PLINTONA VIEW
LONG MDW
LONG MEAD
MEADOW WAY
CROSSWAY
THE MEAD
COURTLAND CRES
BORINGDON CL
JESSOPS
BORINGDON HILL
CLIFTON AVE
CLIFTON CL
BIRKBECK CL
PEACOCK CL
FAIRFIELD
COLEBROOK LA
FARRIERS COTTS
NEWNHAM RD
HUXLEY CL
Boringdon Prim Sch
SCHOOL CL
BAINBRIDGE CT
ORCHARD LA
COLE'S COTTS
DEAN RD
HIGHBURY CRES
Colebrook
TORBRIDGE RD
STRODE RD
Newnham Ind Est
BELL CL
LUCAS LA
HEMERDON WAY
PO
GALLEON CL
LISTER CL
Boringdon Mill Bsns Ctr
TREVERBYN RD
REVELL PARK RD
RAYMOND WAY
LINKADELLS
COLEBROOK RD
HOLBORN PL
1 TORY BROOK AVE
2 TORY BROOK CT
3 WHITEWATER CT
GLENSIDE RISE
DAVID CL
PARKSTONE LA
NEWNHAM WAY
TORRIDGE CL
HEMERDON HTS
TREVERBYN CL
TORY WAY
THE LANE
BORINGDON VILLAS
BORINGDON RD
GLEN RD
PINEWOOD CL
TORRIDGE RD
CHAMBERLAYNE DR
AYLWIN CL
MOORLAND DR
MOORLAND GDNS
GEORGE AVE
MOORLAND AVE
WESTFIELD
EARLS MILL RD
BORINGDON TERR
SWAN GDNS
GREBE CL
ST MARYS CT
HAREWOOD CL
STATION RD
Plympton
Ridgeway Sch
B3416
OLD MILL CT
RIDGE PARK RD
Liby
GEASONS LA
MOORLAND RD
RIDGE PK
DOWNFIELD DR
DOWNFIELD WLK
DOWNFIELD WAY
RIDGEWAY
MALLARD CL
TERN GDNS
HIGHBRIDGE CT
ELM GR
Old Priory Jun Sch
MARKET RD
PRIORY RIDGE
SALTRAM TERR
ST STEPHEN'S PL
MUDGE WAY
OLD PRIORY
PRIORY MILL
PRIORY DR
GEORGE CROSS
POCKLINGTON RISE
CHELMER CL
BEAULY CL
DEVERON
KENMARE DR
LONGBROOK BARTON
DARK STREET LA
GEORGE LA
MANOR PARK CL
WENSUM CL
KENNEL HILL
ROCK TERR
COPSE CL
WILLOW COTTS
UNDERWOOD RD
SYDNEY CL
REDVERS GR
Plympton St Maurice
CHADDLEWOOD CL
FROME CL
HILL CL
WOODSIDE CT
MANOR PARK DR
GRANGE RD
COPSE RD
BARBICAN RD
Longcause Com Specl Sch
DRUNKEN BRIDGE HILL
LONGCAUSE
WAIN PK
WAGGON HILL
NEW PARK RD
SCHOOL LA
CHURCH RD
Dorsmouth Rock
FORE ST
COTTON CL
HELE GDNS
HILLCREST
A
B
C
1
2
3
4
54
55
56
57
58
32
43

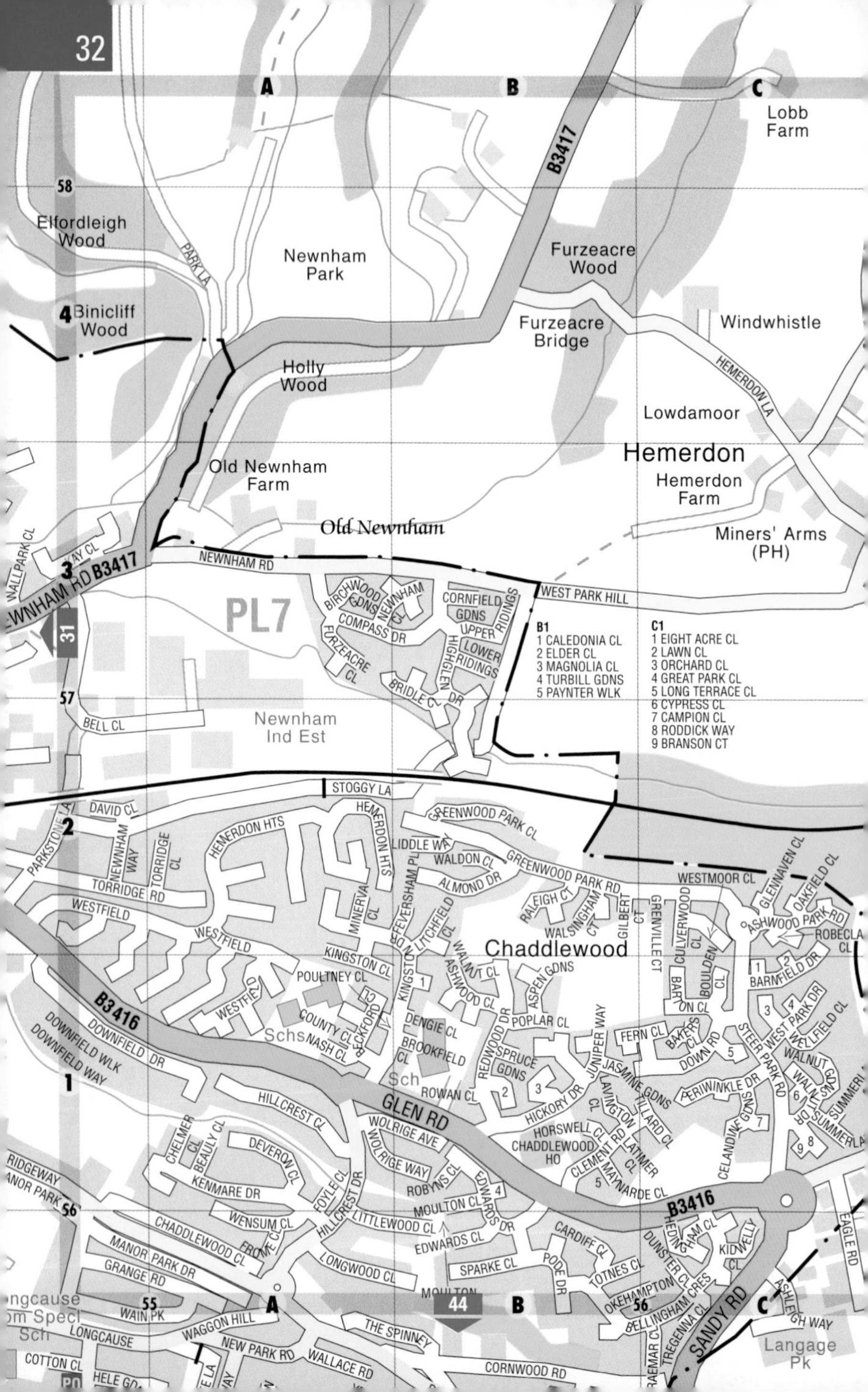
A
B
C
Lobb Farm
B3417
58
Elfordleigh Wood
Newnham Park
PARK LA
Furzeacre Wood
Binicliff Wood
4
Furzeacre Bridge
Windwhistle
Holly Wood
HEMERDON LA
Lowdamoor
Hemerdon
Old Newnham Farm
Hemerdon Farm
Old Newnham
Miners' Arms (PH)
WALLPARK CL
KAY CL
3
NEWNHAM RD B3417
NEWNHAM RD
WEST PARK HILL
PL7
BIRCHWOOD GDNS
NEWNHAM CL
CORNFIELD GDNS
RIDINGS
UPPER
COMPASS DR
LOWER RIDINGS
FURZEACRE CL
HIGHGLEN DR
BRIDLE CL
31
B1
1 CALEDONIA CL
2 ELDER CL
3 MAGNOLIA CL
4 TURBILL GDNS
5 PAYNTER WLK
C1
1 EIGHT ACRE CL
2 LAWN CL
3 ORCHARD CL
4 GREAT PARK CL
5 LONG TERRACE CL
6 CYPRESS CL
7 CAMPION CL
8 RODDICK WAY
9 BRANSON CT
57
BELL CL
Newnham Ind Est
STOGGY LA
DAVID CL
PARKSTONE LA
2
HEMERDON HTS
GREENWOOD PARK CL
LIDDLE WAY
NEWNHAM WAY
TORRIDGE CL
WALDON CL
GREENWOOD PARK RD
TORRIDGE RD
ALMOND DR
WESTMOOR CL
GLENNAVEN CL
OAKFIELD CL
WESTFIELD
MINERVA CL
FEVERSHAM PL
RALEIGH CT
GILBERT CT
GRENVILLE CT
CULVERWOOD CL
ASHWOOD PARK RD
ROBECLA CL
LITCHFIELD CL
WALSINGHAM CT
BOULDEN CL
KINGSTON CL
WALNUT CL
Chaddlewood
BARNFIELD DR
KINGSTON DR
ASHWOOD CL
ASPEN GDNS
BARTON CL
POULTNEY CL
B3416
RECKFORD CL
DENGIE CL
POPLAR CL
WEST PARK DR
WELLFIELD CL
COUNTY CL
JUNIPER WAY
FERN CL
BAKERS CL
DOWNFIELD DR
DOWNFIELD WLK
DOWNFIELD WAY
Schs
NASH CL
BROOKFIELD CL
REDWOOD DR
SPRUCE GDNS
JASMINE GDNS
DOWN RD
STEER PARK RD
WALNUT GDNS
1
Sch
ROWAN CL
HICKORY DR
PERIWINKLE DR
SUMMERLAND
HILLCREST CL
GLEN RD
LAVINGTON CL
TILLARD CL
CELANDINE GDNS
CHELMER CL
BEAULY CL
WOLRIGE AVE
HORSWELL CL
DEVERON CL
WOLRIGE WAY
CHADDLEWOOD HO
CLEMENT RD
LATIMER CL
RIDGEWAY
MANOR PARK
KENMARE DR
FOYLE CL
ROBYNS CL
EDWARDS DR
MAYNARDE CL
56
HILLCREST DR
MOULTON CL
B3416
WENSUM CL
LITTLEWOOD CL
HEDINGHAM CL
EAGLE RD
CHADDLEWOOD CL
FROME CL
EDWARDS CL
CARDIFF CL
DUNSTER CL
KIDWELLY CL
MANOR PARK DR
SPARKE CL
PODE DR
TOTNES CL
GRANGE RD
LONGWOOD CL
ASHLEIGH WAY
Longcause Com Specl Sch
55
WAIN PK
MOULTON
44
OKEHAMPTON CL
BELLINGHAM CRES
TREGENNA CL
SANDY RD
LONGCAUSE
WAGGON HILL
THE SPINNEY
NEW PARK RD
WALLACE RD
COTTON CL
HELE GDNS
CORNWOOD RD
BRAEMAR CL
Langage Pk

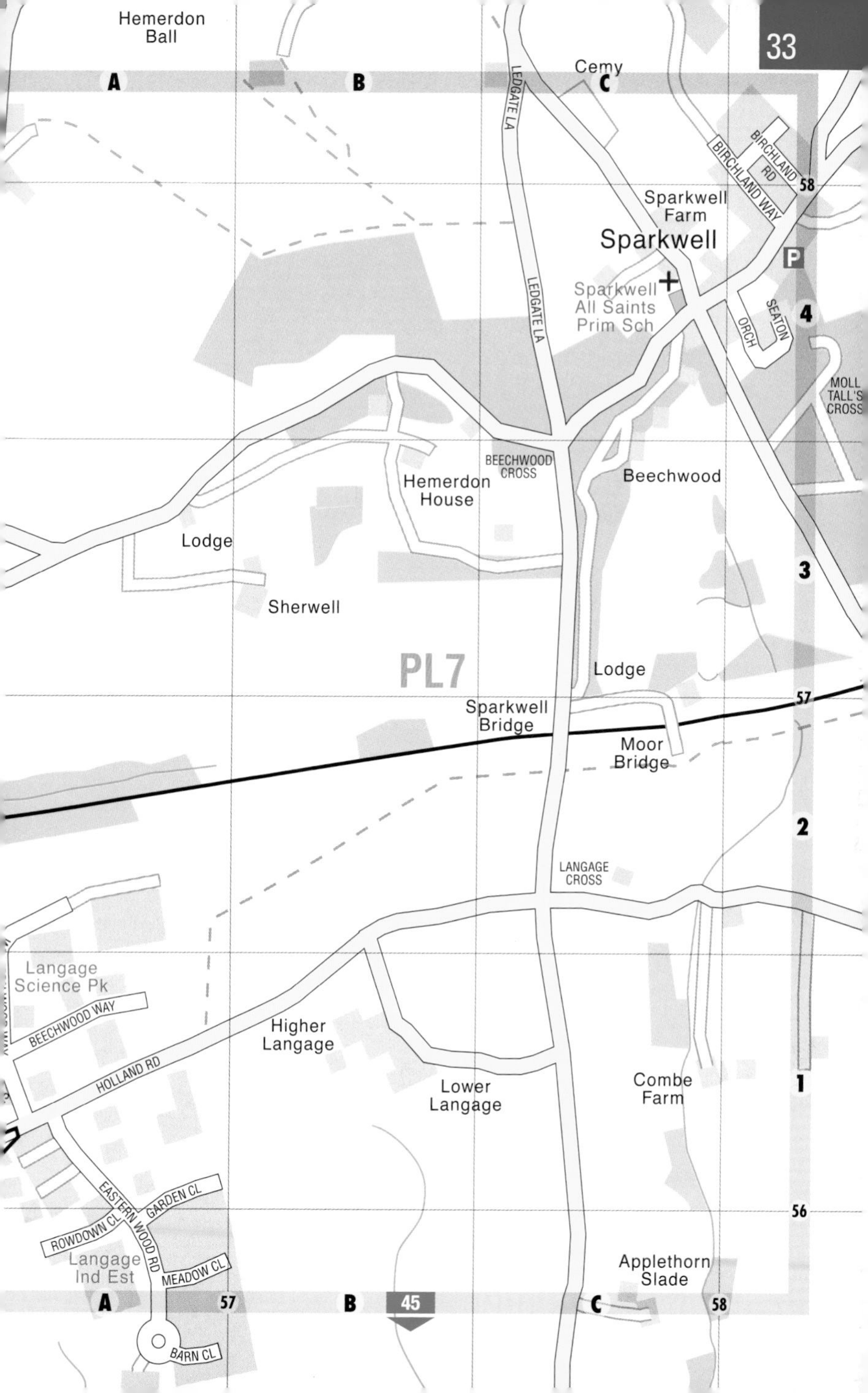
Hemerdon
Ball
A
B
C
Cemy
LEDGATE LA
BIRCHLAND RD
BIRCHLAND WAY
58
Sparkwell
Farm
Sparkwell
Sparkwell
All Saints
Prim Sch
P
SEATON
ORCH
4
MOLL
TALL'S
CROSS
LEDGATE LA
BEECHWOOD
CROSS
Hemerdon
House
Beechwood
Lodge
Sherwell
3
PL7
Lodge
57
Sparkwell
Bridge
Moor
Bridge
2
LANGAGE
CROSS
Langage
Science Pk
BEECHWOOD WAY
Higher
Langage
HOLLAND RD
Lower
Langage
Combe
Farm
1
EASTERN WOOD RD
GARDEN CL
ROWDOWN CL
56
Langage
Ind Est
MEADOW CL
Applethorn
Slade
A
57
B
C
58
BARN CL

45

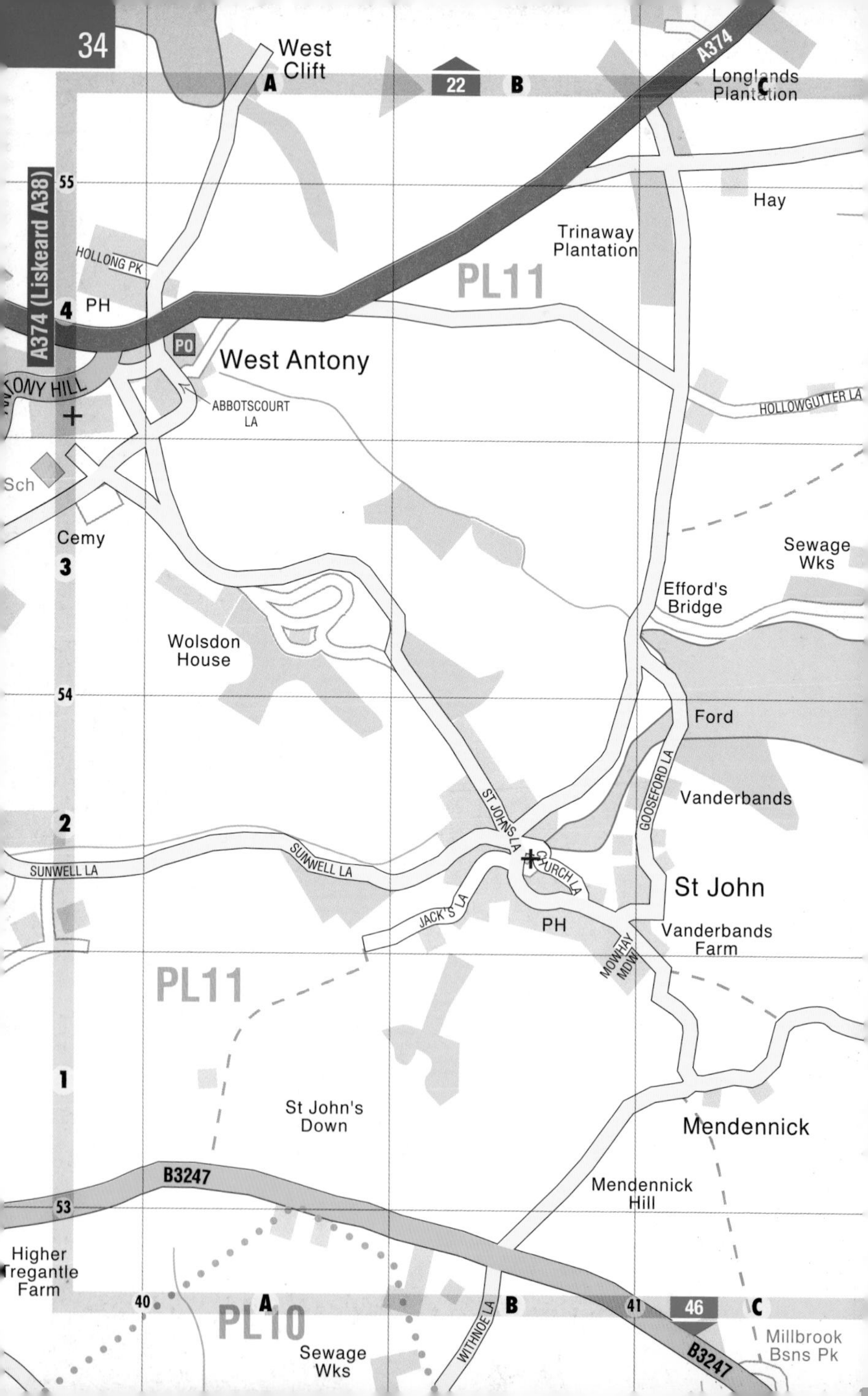
West Clift
A
22
B
C
A374
Longlands Plantation
55
Hay
A374 (Liskeard A38)
HOLLONG PK
Trinaway Plantation
PL11
4
PH
PO
West Antony
ANTONY HILL
ABBOTSCOURT LA
HOLLOWGUTTER LA
Sch
Cemy
3
Sewage Wks
Efford's Bridge
Wolsdon House
54
Ford
GOOSEFORD LA
Vanderbands
ST JOHNS LA
2
SUNWELL LA
SUNWELL LA
CHURCH LA
St John
JACK'S LA
PH
Vanderbands Farm
MOWHAY MDW
PL11
1
St John's Down
Mendennick
B3247
Mendennick Hill
53
Higher Tregantle Farm
40
A
PL10
B
WITHNOE LA
41
46
C
Millbrook Bsns Pk
B3247
Sewage Wks

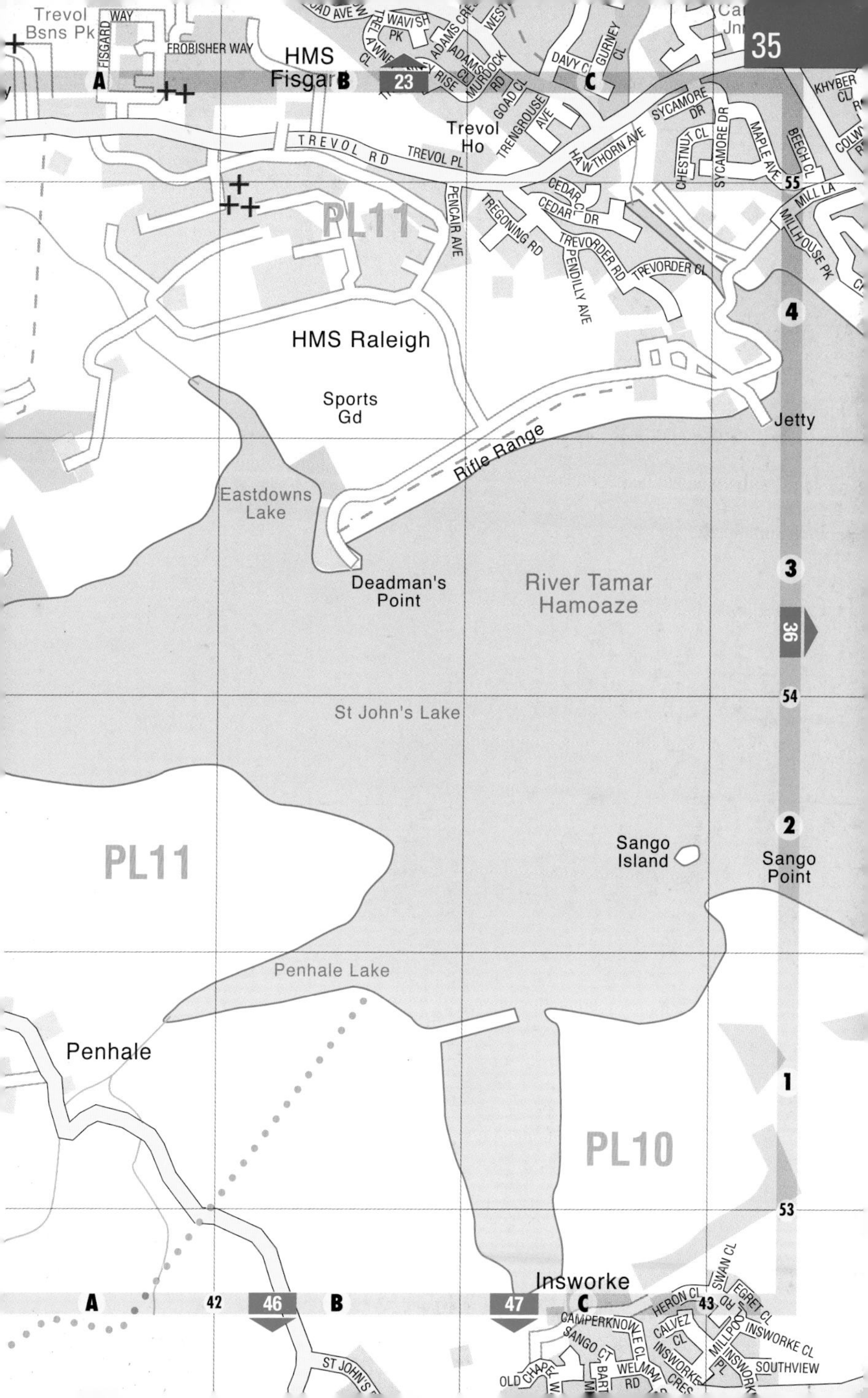
Trevol Bsns Pk
FISGARD WAY
FROBISHER WAY
HMS Fisgard
WAVISH PK
TRELAWNEY
ADAMS CRES
ADAMS CL
MURDOCK RD
GOAD CL
DAVY CL
GURNEY CL
Trevol Ho
TREVOL RD
TREVOL PL
TRENGROUSE AVE
HAWTHORN AVE
SYCAMORE DR
CHESTNUT CL
MAPLE AVE
BEECH CL
KHYBER CL
MILL LA
MILLHOUSE PK
PL11
PENCAIR AVE
TREGONING RD
CEDAR CL
CEDAR DR
TREVORDER RD
TREVORDER CL
PENDILLY AVE
HMS Raleigh
Sports Gd
Jetty
Rifle Range
Eastdowns Lake
Deadman's Point
River Tamar Hamoaze
St John's Lake
Sango Island
Sango Point
PL11
Penhale Lake
Penhale
PL10
Insworke
SWAN CL
EGRET CL
HERON CL
CAMPERKNOWLE CL
CALVEZ CL
MILLPOOL RD
INSWORKE CL
SANGO CT
INSWORKE CRES
INSWORKE PL
SOUTHVIEW
WELMAN RD
OLD CHAPEL
ST JOHN'S
A
B
C
1
2
3
4
23
36
46
47
42
43
53
54
55

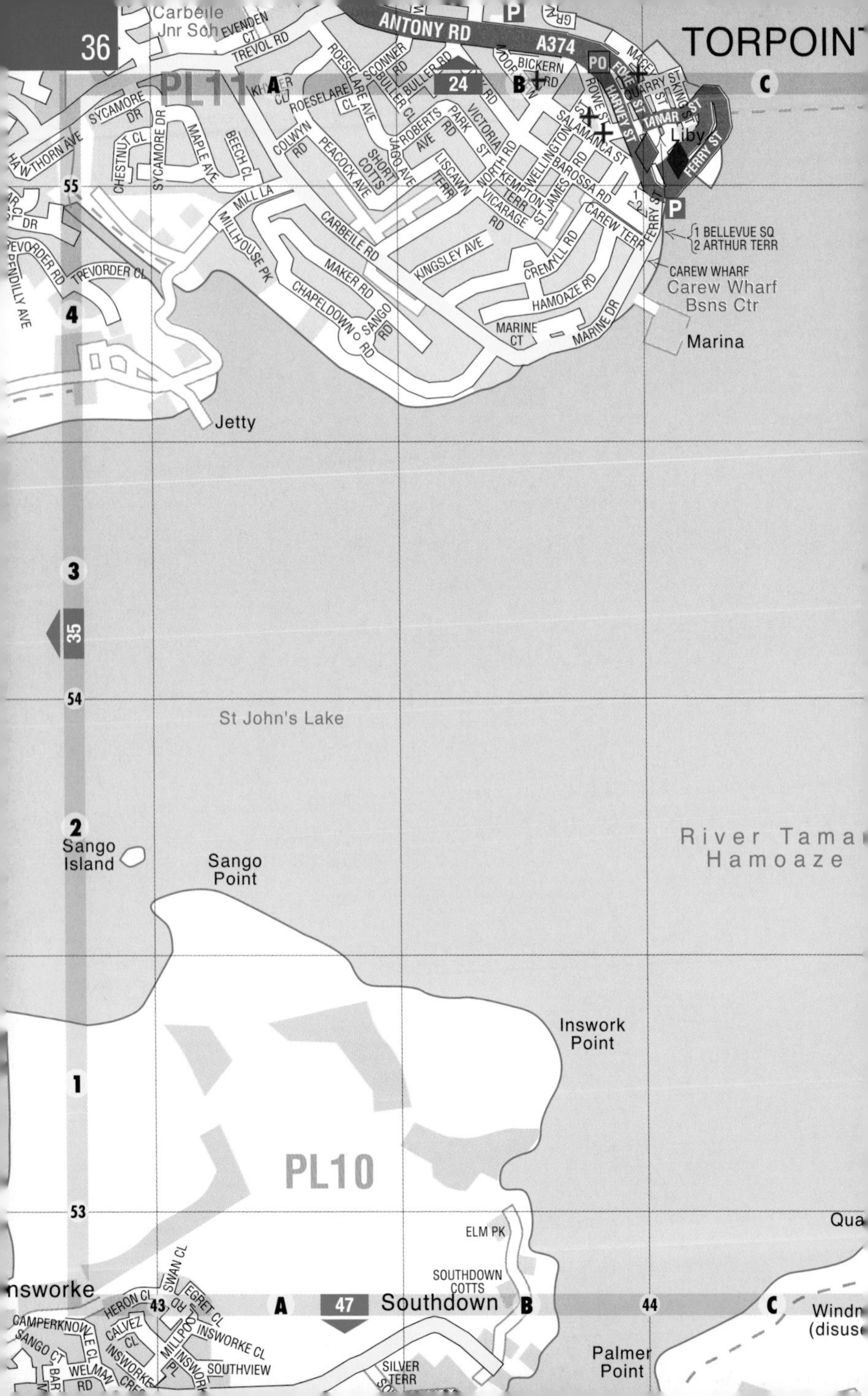
TORPOINT
Carbeile Jnr Sch
EVENDEN CT
TREVOL RD
ANTONY RD
A374
PL11
A
B
C
24
KHYBER CL
ROESELARE AVE
ROESELARE CL
SCONNER RD
BULLER RD
BULLER CL
BICKERN RD
MOOR VIEW
PO
FORE ST
HARVEY ST
ROWE ST
MACEY ST
QUARRY ST
KING ST
TAMAR ST
FERRY ST
Liby
SYCAMORE DR
HAWTHORN AVE
CHESTNUT CL
SYCAMORE DR
MAPLE AVE
BEECH CL
COLWYN RD
PEACOCK AVE
SHORT COTTS
JAGO AVE
ROBERTS AVE
PARK RD
VICTORIA ST
LISCAWN TERR
NORTH RD
KEMPTON TERR
WELLINGTON ST
SALAMANCA ST
BAROSSA RD
ST JAMES RD
VICARAGE RD
CAREW TERR
1 BELLEVUE SQ
2 ARTHUR TERR
CAREW WHARF
Carew Wharf Bsns Ctr
Marina
55
MILL LA
MILLHOUSE PK
CARBEILE RD
KINGSLEY AVE
CREMYLL RD
HAMOAZE RD
MARINE CT
MARINE DR
MAKER RD
CHAPELDOWN RD
SANGO RD
TREVORDER CL
TREVORDER RD
PENDILLY AVE
4
Jetty
3
35
54
St John's Lake
2
Sango Island
Sango Point
River Tamar
Hamoaze
Inswork Point
1
PL10
53
ELM PK
SOUTHDOWN COTTS
Qua
Insworke
SWAN CL
EGRET CL
HERON CL
43
A
47
Southdown
B
44
C
Windm (disus
CAMPERKNOWLE CL
SANGO CT
CALVEZ CL
INSWORKE CL
MILLPOOL
SOUTHVIEW
WELMAN RD
SILVER TERR
Palmer Point

37
PLYMOUTH
Moon Cove
Ferry V
TAMAR WHARF
TAMAR ST
JOHN ST
POTTERY RD
A374
FERRY RD
25
Parkside Com Tech Coll
MILNE PL
EXMOUTH RD
ACRE PL
NAPIER ST
TRAFALGAR PLACE
DEVONPORT RD
STOPFORD PL
NELSON AVE
ACRE COTTS
SOUTH HILL
FITZROY RD
Riverside Bsns Pk
NEW PASSAGE HILL
WRIGHT CL
PARK AVE
DURRANT CL
PORTEOUS CL
KNOWLAND CL
WATERLOO ST
ALBEMARLE VILLAS
WELLINGTON ST
PROVIDENCE PL
KINGS CT
Morice Town
Sch
QUEEN ST
MORICE ST
ST AUBYN RD
MARLBOROUGH ROW
MARLBOROUGH ST
GRANBY GN
GRANBY ST
KEYES CL
PARADISE RD
PARADISE PL
55
RIVERSIDE PL 1
CHAPMANS OPE 2
MORICE SQ 3
ASHBOURNE CL 4
GRANBY PL 5
ORDNANCE ST
HAMOAZE PL
CANNON ST
CORNWALL BEACH
CORNWALL ST
HOLMANS BLDGS
ALBANY ST
GRANBY WAY
PO
GRANBY CT
ST NAZAIRE CL
FORE ST
YORK ST
RAGLAN RD
KINGS RD
Plymouth Coll of F Ed
Coll
COREA TERR
RECTORY RD
FIRST AVE
SECOND AVE
THIRD AVE
1 PRINCES ST
2 LOFOTEN CL
3 VAAGSO CL
4 DIEPPE CL
5 ST NAZAIRE APP
6 ST THERESE'S CT
Quay Landing Stage
St Joseph's RC Prim Sch
CHAPEL ST
BARRACK ST
The Brickfields (Recn Gd)
PL1
ST AUBYN ST
KER ST
STOPE
MILLS RD
MADDEN RD
BRICKFIELDS CL
DAMEREL CL
KING'S RD
WATERLOO CT
CUMBERLAND RD
DEVONPORT HILL
A374
STONEHOUSE BRIDGE
TAMAR HO
DUNCAN ST
DUKE ST
CURTIS ST
EDINBURGH ST
BENNETT ST
MOUNT ST
PEMBROKE LA
PEMBROKE ST
GEORGE ST
1 CUMBERLAND ST
2 MONUMENT ST
3 RAGLAN GDNS
4 RAGLAN CT
5 THEATRE OPE
6 GEORGE SQ
7 SUTTON CT
RICHMOND WLK
NEWPORT ST
Mount Wise Com Prim Sch
JAMES ST
CLOWANCE LA
STEPHEN ST
CLOWANCE ST
CLOWANCE CL
MOUNT WISE CT
BAKERS PL
3
STONEHALL
CREMYLL ST
38
PROSPECT ROW
ST MICHAEL'S CL
LOCKS WLK
GARRISON CL
Mon
Mount Wise
Mount Wise Park
Admiraly House
RICHMOND WLK
DURNFORD STREET
54
THE QUARTERDECK
ST
STRAND
Mutton Cove
OCEAN CT
Marina
TELEGRAPH WHARF
2
Ferry P
PL1
PH
Devil's Point
ADMIRALTY COTTS
The Narrows
Obelisk
ST JULIAN'S COTTS
Cremyll
1
Western King Point
Wilderness Point
Blockhouse
B3247
PL10
Empacombe Cottage
Empacombe
53
Barn Pool
A
45
B
C
46
Home Farm
Barrow Park
Mount Edgcumbe

Prim Sch
Stuart Road Prim Sch
Pennycomequick
STUART RD
PO
A
B
C
26
STOPFORD PL
NELSON AVE
COLLINGWOOD RD
VALLETORT RD
STUART RD
MERSTON ST
ST BARNABAS TERR
SOUTH HILL
FITZROY RD
WATERLOO ST
WILTON ST
HOTHAM PL
QUEEN'S GATE
ARUNDEL CRES
NORTH RD W
EXMOUTH
ALBEMARLE VILLAS
WELLINGTON ST
PROVIDENCE PL
KINGS CT
JAN CT
VALLETORT LA
WILTON RD
Victoria Park
PATNA PL
ILBERT ST
PENROSE ST
SYDNEY
55
PARADISE RD
PARADISE PL
FELLOWES PL
EDGCUMBE AVE
MILL BRIDGE
CECIL ST
Plymouth Coll of F Ed
Devonport High Sch for Boys
ELDAD HILL
WYNDHAM LA
WYNDHAM ST E
Cath
HARWELL ST
HASTINGS T
KINGS RD
Coll
COREA TERR
FIRST AVE
SECOND AVE
RECTORY RD
THIRD AVE
PL1
THE MEWS
54
ANSTIS ST
Sch
CECIL ST
FRANCIS ST
NESWICK ST
WESTERN A
4
The Brickfields (Recn Gd)
KING'S RD
WATERLOO YARD FLATS
VALLETORT FLATS
THE SQUARE
St Dunstan's Abbey Plymouth Coll Jun Sch
STOKE RD
KING ST
St Peters CE Prim Sch
VALLETORT PL
WATERLOO CL
WATERLOO CT
HIGH ST
CLARENCE PL
MANOR ST
ALICE ST
OCTAGON ST
RENDLE ST
DAMEREL CL
PEEL ST
ADELAIDE LA
UNION PL
MANOR GDNS
A374 DEVONPORT HILL
STONEHOUSE BRIDGE
EDGCUMBE ST
UNION ST
A374
HIGH ST & WATERLOO ST FLATS
MKT ST
MARKET CL
EAST ST
STONEHOUSE ST
GEORGE PL
SAWREY ST
MARTIN ST
BATH LA
BATH ST
THE CRESCENT
RICHMOND WLK
NEWPORT ST
Stonehouse
3
BARRACK PL
DURNFORD ST
EMMA PL
MILLBAY RD
St Andrew's CE Prim Sch
BAKERS PL
STONEHALL FLATS
CREMYLL ST
37
Admiralty House
1 EMMA PLACE OPE
2 MARKET ST
3 COBBLESTONE LA
Millbay Docks
WEST HOE RD
Millbay
CITA
DURNFORD STREET OPE
Barracks
RICHMOND WLK
54
ADMIRAL'S HARD
STRAND ST
THE QUARTERDECK
55
TA Ctr
WALKER TERR
Ferryport
CLIFF RD
OCEAN CT
Marina
POUND ST
ADMIRALTY ST
TELEGRAPH WHARF
CAMBER RD
PIER ST
WEST HOE RD
GREAT WESTERN RD
2
FREEMANS WHARF
Millbay Docks
West Hoe
GRAND PAR
THE MANSION HO
ST PAUL ST
St George's CE Prim Sch
Ferry P
PL1
MOUNT STONE RD
ROYAL WILLIAM RD
ADMIRALTY RD
55
Tower
Devil's Point
ADMIRALTY COTTS
Eastern King Point
Firestone Bay
The Narrows
1
Western King Point
53
Mast
46
A
B
PL1
47
C
Drakes or St Nicholas's Island
The Bridge

GLEN
NORTH RD E
CLIFTON PL
NORTH HILL
GREENBANK RD
SEA VIEW AVE
ROSEBERY RD
DURHAM
SALTASH RD
A386
A
B
27
C
Univ
Coll
ETON PL
JOHN LA
JAMES ST
Univ of Plymouth
B3250
ARMADA ST
BARING ST
B3238
WOODSIDE
CHADDLEWOOD AVE
SEYMOUR AVE
CECIL AVE
CRAVEN AVE
Sch
55
A374
COBOURG ST
GLANVILLE ST
DRAKE CIR
TAVISTOCK PL
GIBBON LA
GIBBONS ST
Mus & Art Gal
Liby
Mount Street Prim Sch
CAMDEN ST
LIPSON RD
MAY TERR
TOTHILL AVE
GREENBANK AVE
BEATRICE AVE
WATTS RD
SOUTH
MAYFLOWER ST
NORTH ST
REGENT ST
PL1
EGERTON RD
CLEVELAND
4
KNIGHTON RD
CHARLES ST
Univ
EBRINGTON ST
BEAUMONT RD
CORNWALL ST
ARMADA WAY
drakecircus
HILL ST
Holy Cross RC Prim Sch
TOTHILL RD
DESBOROUGH RD
St Jude's
EXETER ST
B3238
CROMWELL RD
ROYAL PAR
BRETON SIDE
Guildhall
HOW ST
LOOE ST
C Ctr
Ct
Ct
Mus
BUCKWELL ST
B3240
Univ
SUTTON RD
ST JOHN'S RD
SHAPTERS RD
ST LEO
PRINCESS ST
NOTTE ST
VAUXHALL ST
Barbican
Sutton Harbour
CLARE PL
CATTEDOWN RD
3
FRED ST
LOCKYER ST
Univ of Plymouth
HOE APP
SOUTHSIDE ST
QUAY RD
COMMERCIAL RD
BARBICAN APP
40
CITADEL RD E
Swing Bridge
Aquarium
HOE RD
Mus
LAMBHAY HILL
TEATS HILL RD
CLOVELLY RD
54
THE PROMENADE
The Hoe
Smeaton Tower
Royal Citadel
Coxside
Cattedown
HOE RD
MADEIRA RD
2
55
57
CATTEDOWN RD
Esso Wharf
SPINNAKER QUAY
Mount Batten Breakwater
Clovelly Bay
1
Mount Batten Tower
PL9
Mount Batten Point
Ferry P (Summer Only)
SHAW WAY
Quay
SHAW WAY
Mount Batten Waterside Pk
53
LAWRENCE RD
LORD LOUIS CRES
CATALINA VILLAS
DURWENT CL
A
48
B
C
49
Batten Bay
STAMFORD FORT COTTS
Dunstone Point
FORD LA

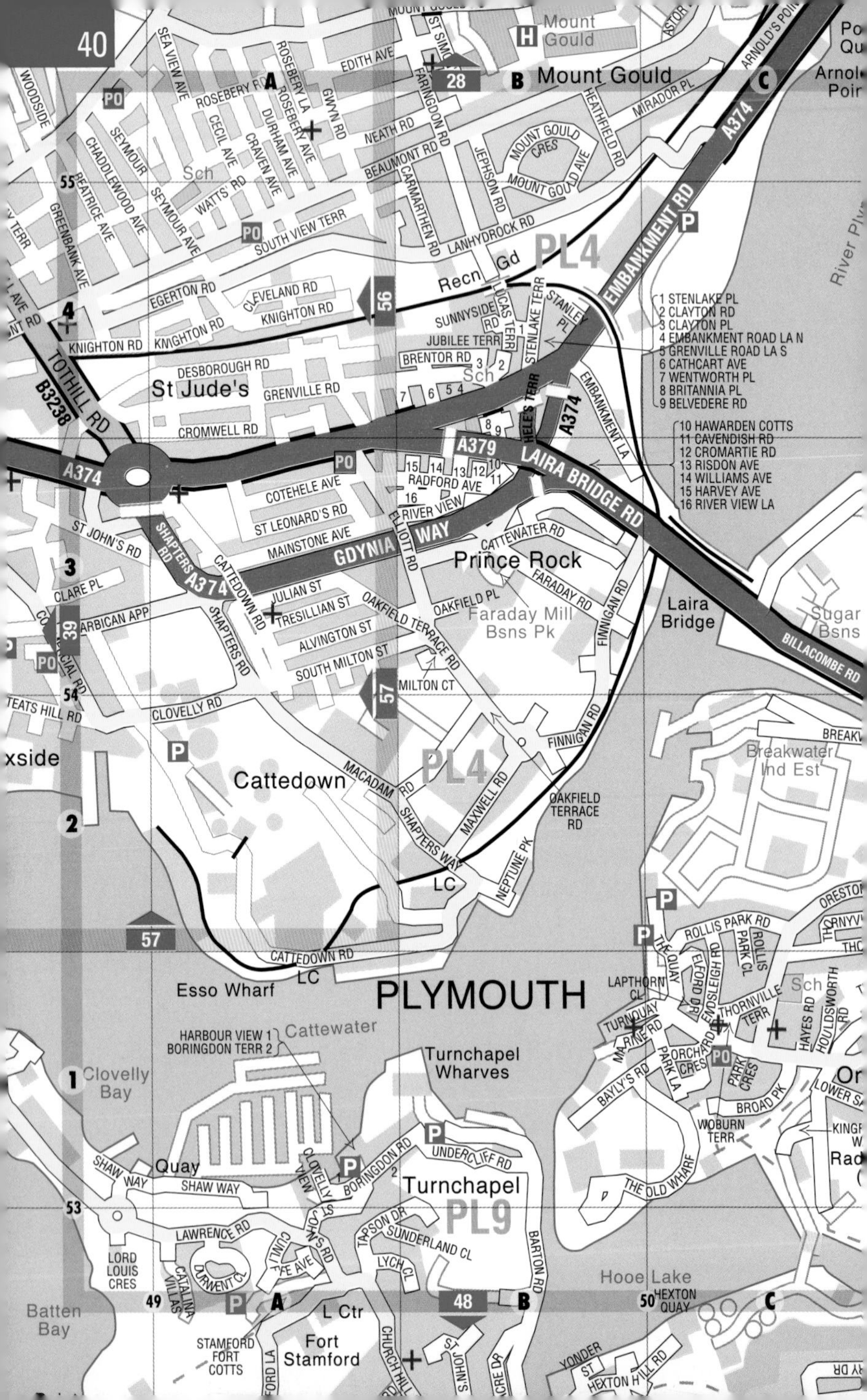

Mount Gould
Plymouth
PL4
PL9
St Jude's
Prince Rock
Cattedown
Laira Bridge
Turnchapel
Turnchapel Wharves
Esso Wharf
Cattewater
Clovelly Bay
Batten Bay
Hooe Lake
Fort Stamford
Faraday Mill Bsns Pk
Breakwater Ind Est
Recn Gd
EMBANKMENT RD
LAIRA BRIDGE RD
GDYNIA WAY
TOTHILL RD
CATTEDOWN RD
A374
A379
B3238
1 STENLAKE PL
2 CLAYTON RD
3 CLAYTON PL
4 EMBANKMENT ROAD LA N
5 GRENVILLE ROAD LA S
6 CATHCART AVE
7 WENTWORTH PL
8 BRITANNIA PL
9 BELVEDERE RD
10 HAWARDEN COTTS
11 CAVENDISH RD
12 CROMARTIE RD
13 RISDON AVE
14 WILLIAMS AVE
15 HARVEY AVE
16 RIVER VIEW LA
HARBOUR VIEW 1
BORINGDON TERR 2

28 56 57 39 48

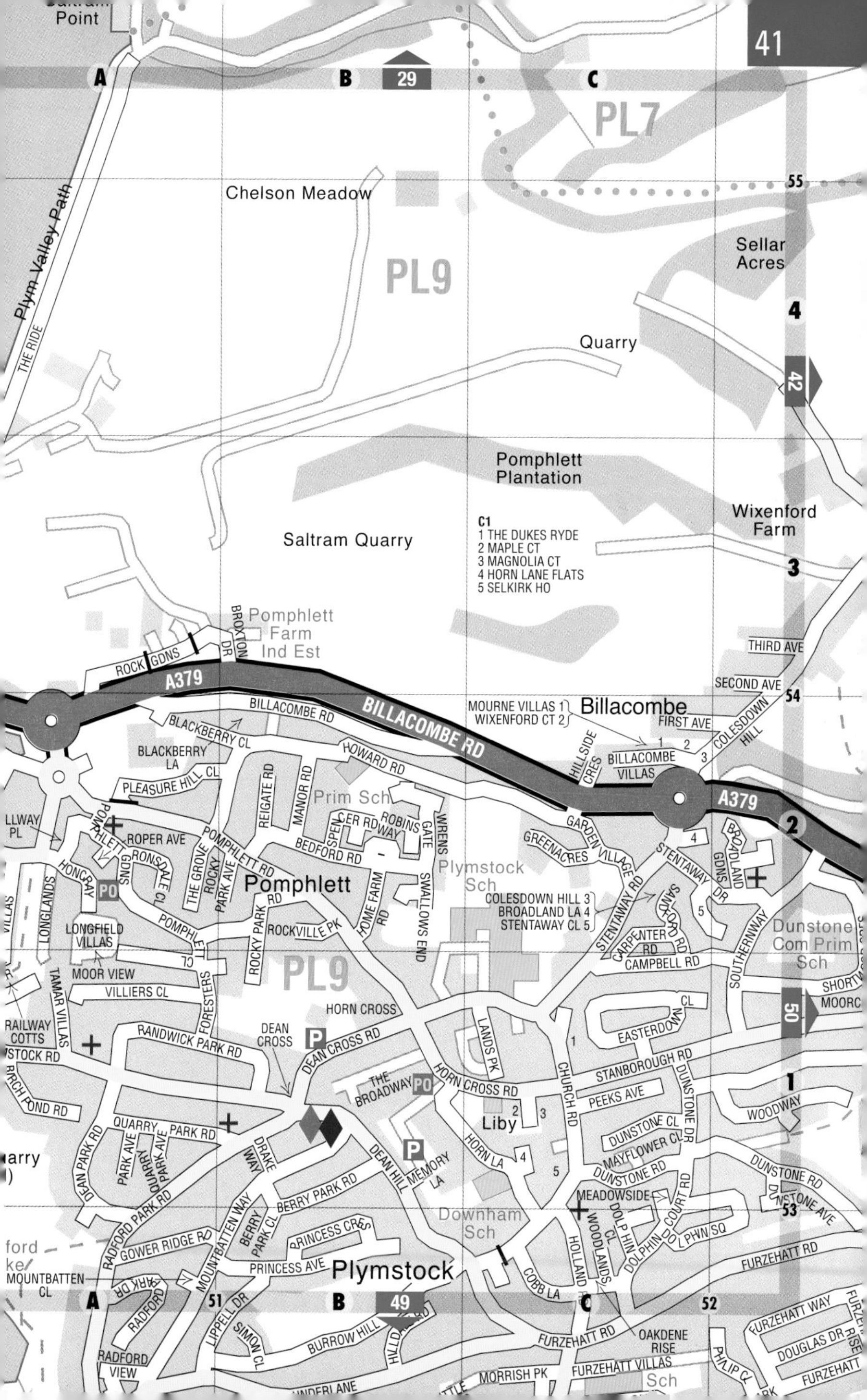

Point
A
B
29
C
PL7
55
Chelson Meadow
Plym Valley Path
PL9
Sellar Acres
4
THE RIDE
Quarry
42
Pomphlett Plantation
Wixenford Farm
Saltram Quarry
C1
1 THE DUKES RYDE
2 MAPLE CT
3 MAGNOLIA CT
4 HORN LANE FLATS
5 SELKIRK HO
3
Pomphlett Farm Ind Est
BROXTON DR
ROCK GDNS
A379
THIRD AVE
SECOND AVE
54
BILLACOMBE RD
MOURNE VILLAS 1
WIXENFORD CT 2
Billacombe
FIRST AVE
COLESDOWN HILL
BLACKBERRY CL
BLACKBERRY LA
HOWARD RD
HILLSIDE CRES
BILLACOMBE VILLAS
PLEASURE HILL CL
REIGATE RD
MANOR RD
Prim Sch
A379
POMPHLETT GDNS
ROPER AVE
SPENCER RD
ROBINS WAY
WRENS GATE
GARDEN VILLAGE
BROADLAND GDNS
2
RONSDALE CL
POMPHLETT RD
BEDFORD RD
GREENACRES
STENTAWAY DR
HONGRAY
PO
THE GROVE
ROCKY PARK AVE
Pomphlett
Plymstock Sch
SWALLOWS END
STENTAWAY RD
SAMFORD RD
ROCKY PARK RD
HOME FARM RD
COLESDOWN HILL 3
BROADLAND LA 4
STENTAWAY CL 5
SOUTHERNWAY
Dunstone Com Prim Sch
LONGLANDS
LONGFIELD VILLAS
POMPHLETT CL
ROCKVILLE PK
CARPENTER RD
CAMPBELL RD
TAMAR VILLAS
MOOR VIEW
VILLIERS CL
PL9
FORESTERS
HORN CROSS
EASTERDOWN CL
50
RAILWAY COTTS
RANDWICK PARK RD
DEAN CROSS
P
DEAN CROSS RD
LANDS PK
STANBOROUGH RD
1
THE BROADWAY
PO
HORN CROSS RD
CHURCH RD
PEEKS AVE
WOODWAY
DUNSTONE DR
POND RD
QUARRY PARK RD
Liby
DUNSTONE CL
DEAN PARK RD
PARK AVE
QUARRY PARK AVE
DRAKE WAY
DEAN HILL
P
MEMORY LA
HORN LA
MAYFLOWER CL
DUNSTONE RD
DUNSTONE RD
DUNSTONE AVE
53
RADFORD PARK RD
BERRY PARK RD
MEADOWSIDE
COURT RD
DOLPHIN CL
MOUNTBATTEN WAY
BERRY PARK CL
Downham Sch
DOLPHIN SQ
WOODLANDS
GOWER RIDGE RD
PRINCESS CRES
HOLLAND RD
FURZEHATT RD
MOUNTBATTEN CL
PRINCESS AVE
Plymstock
COBB LA
PARK DR
A
51
B
49
C
52
RADFORD
LIPPELL DR
FURZEHATT WAY
SIMON CL
BURROW HILL
FURZEHATT RD
OAKDENE RISE
DOUGLAS DR
FURZEHATT RISE
RADFORD VIEW
MORRISH PK
FURZEHATT VILLAS
Sch
PHILIP CL
FURZEHATT

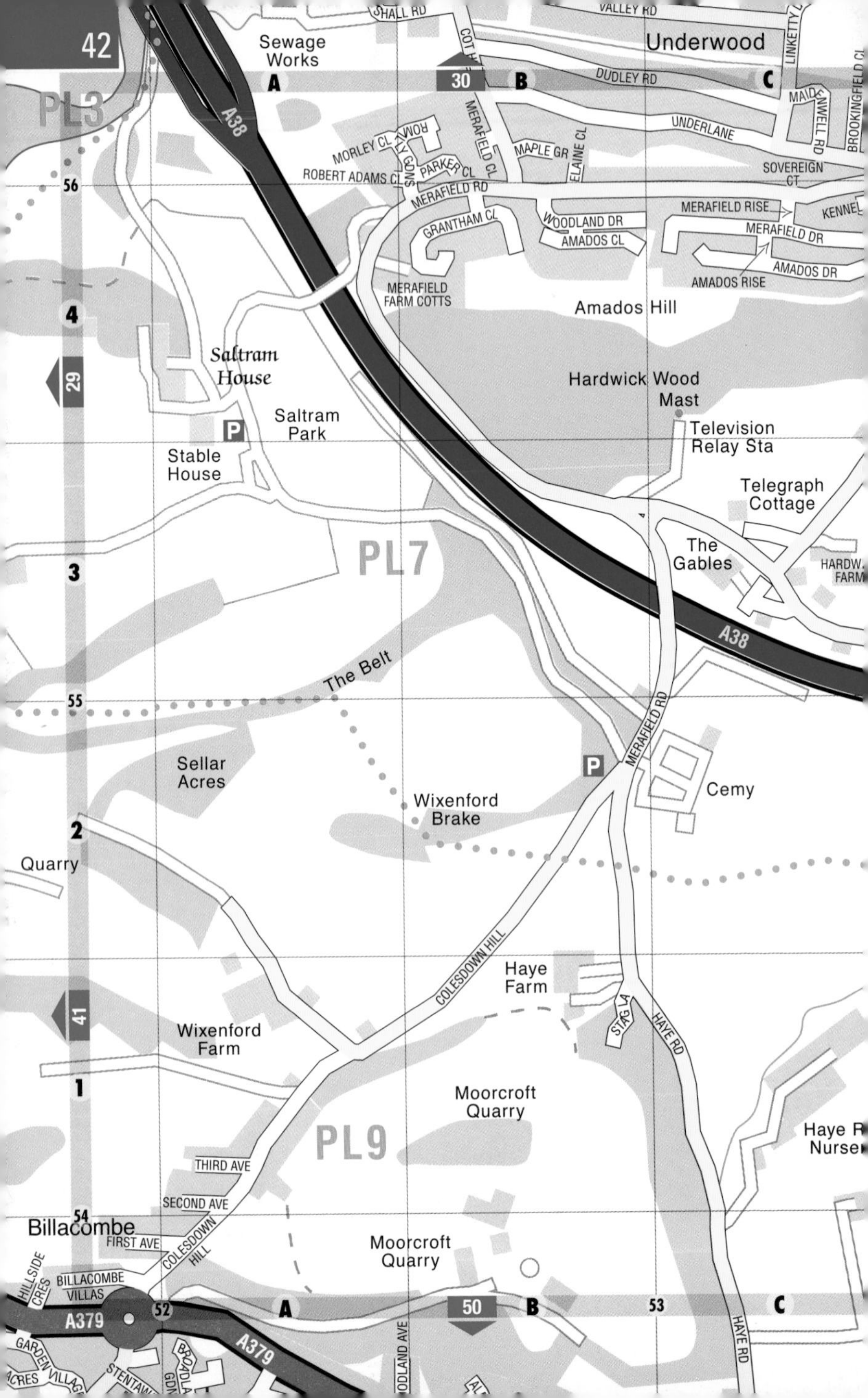

PL3
PL7
PL9
Sewage Works
Underwood
VALLEY RD
DUDLEY RD
UNDERLANE
MORLEY CL
ROBERT ADAMS CL
PARKER CL
MERAFIELD CL
MAPLE GR
ELAINE CL
SOVEREIGN CT
MERAFIELD RD
GRANTHAM CL
WOODLAND DR
AMADOS CL
MERAFIELD RISE
KENNEL
MERAFIELD DR
AMADOS DR
AMADOS RISE
MAIDENWELL RD
BROOKINGFIELD CL
MERAFIELD FARM COTTS
Amados Hill
Hardwick Wood
Mast
Television Relay Sta
Telegraph Cottage
The Gables
Saltram House
Saltram Park
Stable House
A38
The Belt
Sellar Acres
Wixenford Brake
Cemy
Quarry
COLESDOWN HILL
Haye Farm
STAG LA
HAYE RD
Wixenford Farm
Moorcroft Quarry
Haye R
Nurser
THIRD AVE
SECOND AVE
FIRST AVE
Billacombe
HILLSIDE CRES
BILLACOMBE VILLAS
A379
GARDEN VILLAGE
ACRES
STENTAWAY
BROADLAND GDNS
WOODLAND AVE
A
B
C
30
29
41
50
56
55
54
52
53
4
3
2
1

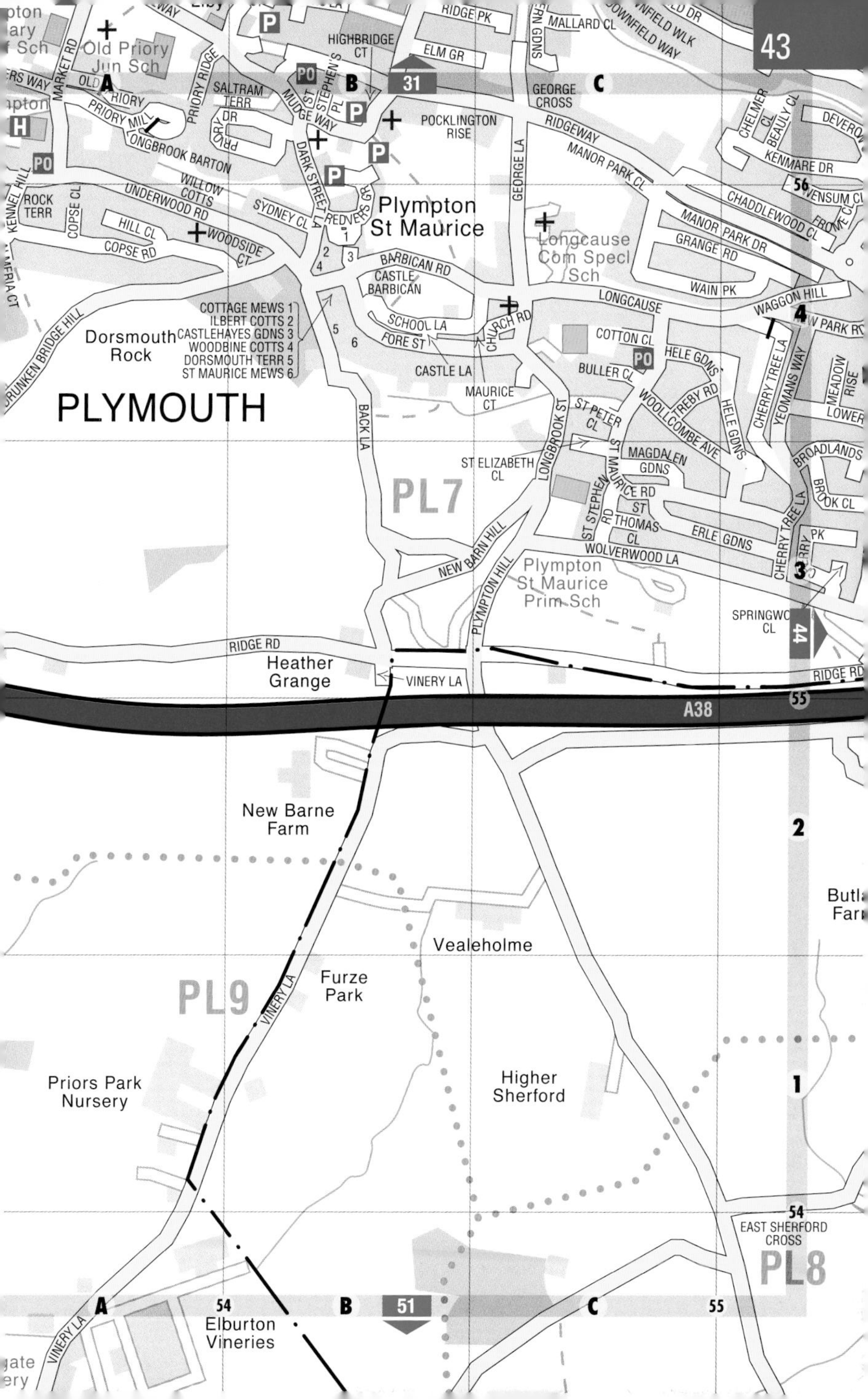
PLYMOUTH
Plympton
St Maurice
PL7
PL9
PL8
Old Priory
Jun Sch
Dorsmouth
Rock
Longcause
Com Specl
Sch
Plympton
St Maurice
Prim Sch
Heather
Grange
New Barne
Farm
Vealeholme
Furze
Park
Higher
Sherford
Priors Park
Nursery
Elburton
Vineries
EAST SHERFORD
CROSS
HIGHBRIDGE
CT
RIDGE PK
MALLARD CL
ELM GR
GEORGE
CROSS
POCKLINGTON
RISE
RIDGEWAY
MANOR PARK CL
CHADDLEWOOD CL
MANOR PARK DR
GRANGE RD
WAIN PK
KENMARE DR
CHELMER CL
BEAULY CL
WENSUM CL
FROME CL
WAGGON HILL
LONGCAUSE
OLD PRIORY
PRIORY MILL
LONGBROOK BARTON
SALTRAM
TERR
PRIORY DR
PRIORY RIDGE
MARKET RD
MUDGE WAY
ST STEPHEN'S PL
DARK STREET LA
REDVERS GR
WILLOW
COTTS
UNDERWOOD RD
SYDNEY CL
ROCK
TERR
KENNEL HILL
COPSE CL
HILL CL
COPSE RD
WOODSIDE
CT
BARBICAN RD
CASTLE
BARBICAN
SCHOOL LA
FORE ST
CHURCH RD
CASTLE LA
MAURICE
CT
COTTAGE MEWS 1
ILBERT COTTS 2
CASTLEHAYES GDNS 3
WOODBINE COTTS 4
DORSMOUTH TERR 5
ST MAURICE MEWS 6
DRUNKEN BRIDGE HILL
GEORGE LA
COTTON CL
BULLER CL
HELE GDNS
TREBY RD
WOOLLCOMBE AVE
CHERRY TREE LA
YEOMANS WAY
MEADOW
RISE
LOWER
BROADLANDS
BROOK CL
ST PETER
CL
ST ELIZABETH
CL
LONGBROOK ST
ST MAURICE RD
MAGDALEN
GDNS
ST STEPHEN RD
ST
THOMAS
CL
ERLE GDNS
WOLVERWOOD LA
NEW BARN HILL
PLYMPTON HILL
BACK LA
SPRINGWO
CL
RIDGE RD
VINERY LA
A38
31
44
51
55
54
56
A
B
C
1
2
3
4

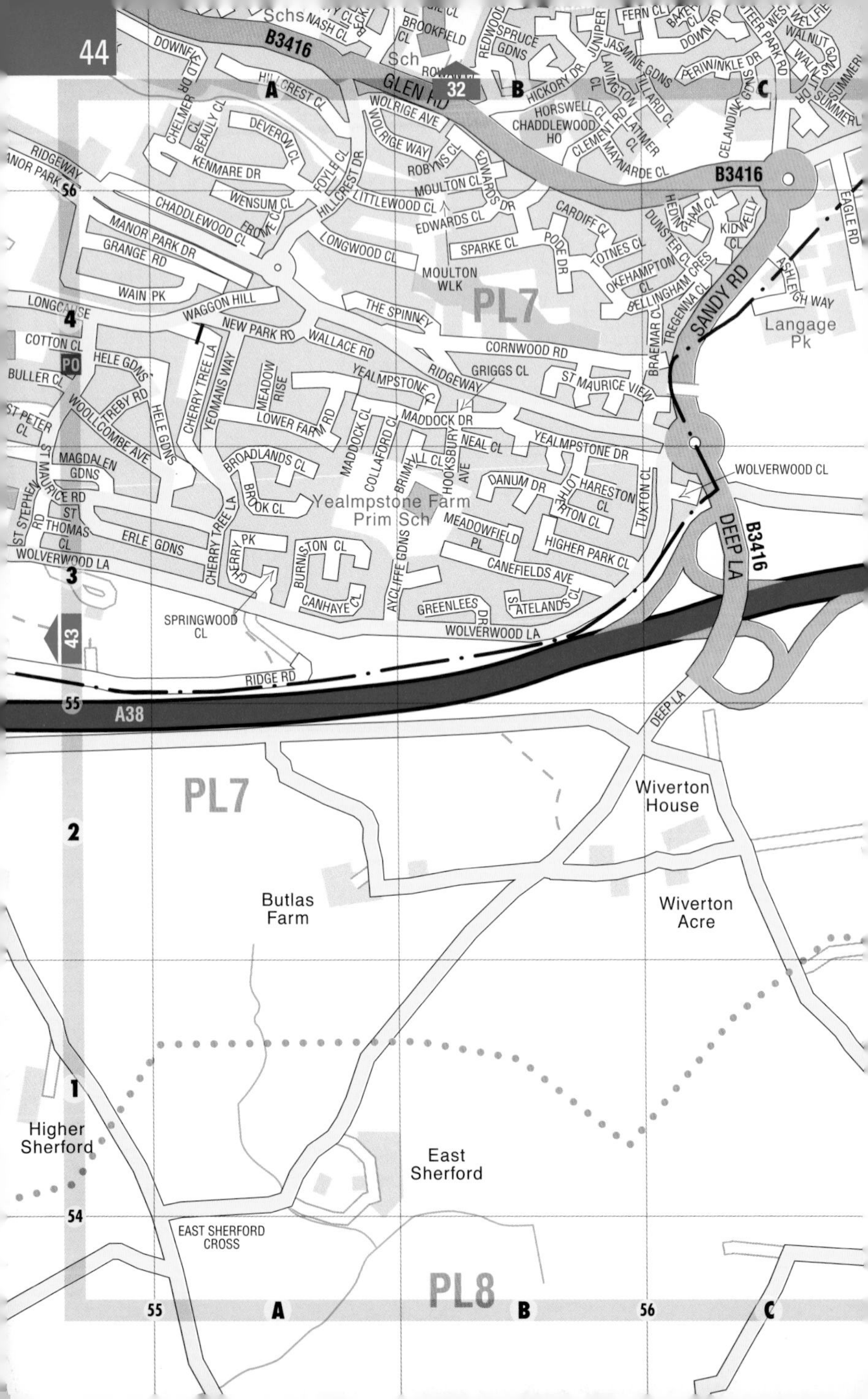

B3416
GLEN RD
32
A
B
C
PL7
Yealmpstone Farm Prim Sch
Langage Pk
SANDY RD
DEEP LA
A38
RIDGEWAY
WAGGON HILL
NEW PARK RD
WALLACE RD
CORNWOOD RD
YEALMPSTONE DR
WOLVERWOOD LA
RIDGE RD
CHADDLEWOOD CL
MANOR PARK DR
GRANGE RD
WAIN PK
LONGCAUSE
COTTON CL
BULLER CL
WOOLLCOMBE AVE
CHERRY TREE LA
YEOMANS WAY
LOWER FARM RD
MADDOCK DR
WOLVERWOOD CL
SPRINGWOOD CL
43
55
56
PL7
Wiverton House
Butlas Farm
Wiverton Acre
Higher Sherford
East Sherford
EAST SHERFORD CROSS
PL8
54
4
3
2
1

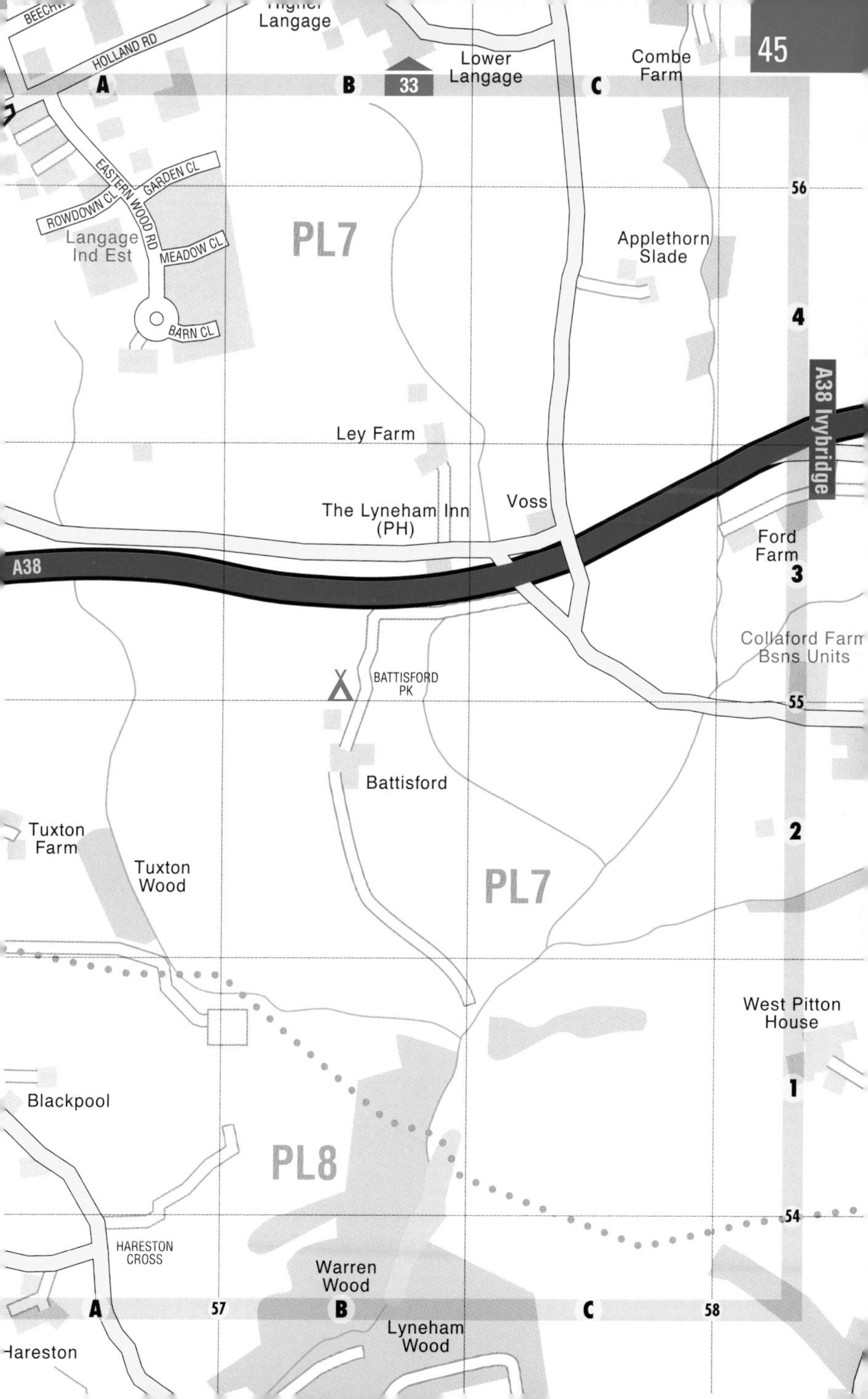
BEECH...
HOLLAND RD
Higher Langage
Lower Langage
33
Combe Farm
A
B
C
EASTERN WOOD RD
GARDEN CL
ROWDOWN CL
MEADOW CL
BARN CL
Langage Ind Est
PL7
Applethorn Slade
56
4
A38 Ivybridge
Ley Farm
The Lyneham Inn (PH)
Voss
A38
Ford Farm
3
Collaford Farm Bsns Units
BATTISFORD PK
55
Battisford
Tuxton Farm
Tuxton Wood
2
PL7
West Pitton House
Blackpool
1
PL8
54
HARESTON CROSS
Warren Wood
A
57
B
C
58
Lyneham Wood
Hareston

34
35
A
B
C
Penhale
Mendennick
Mendennick Hill
PL11
53
B3247
Works
4
Millbrook Bsns Pk
ST JOHN'S RD
TREFU TER
POTTERY EST
ST JOHN'S CL
PL10
Millbrook CE Prim Sch
New Barn
PRIESTHOOD TERR
BLINDWELL HILL
LAKE MEWS
NEWPORT
3
BRAKE LA
Blindwell
MOUNT PLEASANT
NEW ST
PH
Millbrook Resr
RICHARDS TERR 1
THE PARADE 2
KNILL CROSS COTTS 3
FORE ST
DAWES LA
PO
KING ST
ST ANDREWS ST
WEST ST
Higher Hounster Farm
52
HOUNSTER DR
WELL'S CT
P
MILLPOOL HEAD
HOUNSTER HILL
RADFORD LA
Tregonhawke Farm
Dadbrook
2
Tregonhawke
Whitsand Bay Holiday Pk
DONKEY LA
Treninnow Grove
1
Treninnow
PL10
MILITARY RD
51
TRENINNOW & WIGGLE CHALETS
Whitsand Bay
41
42
Wiggle

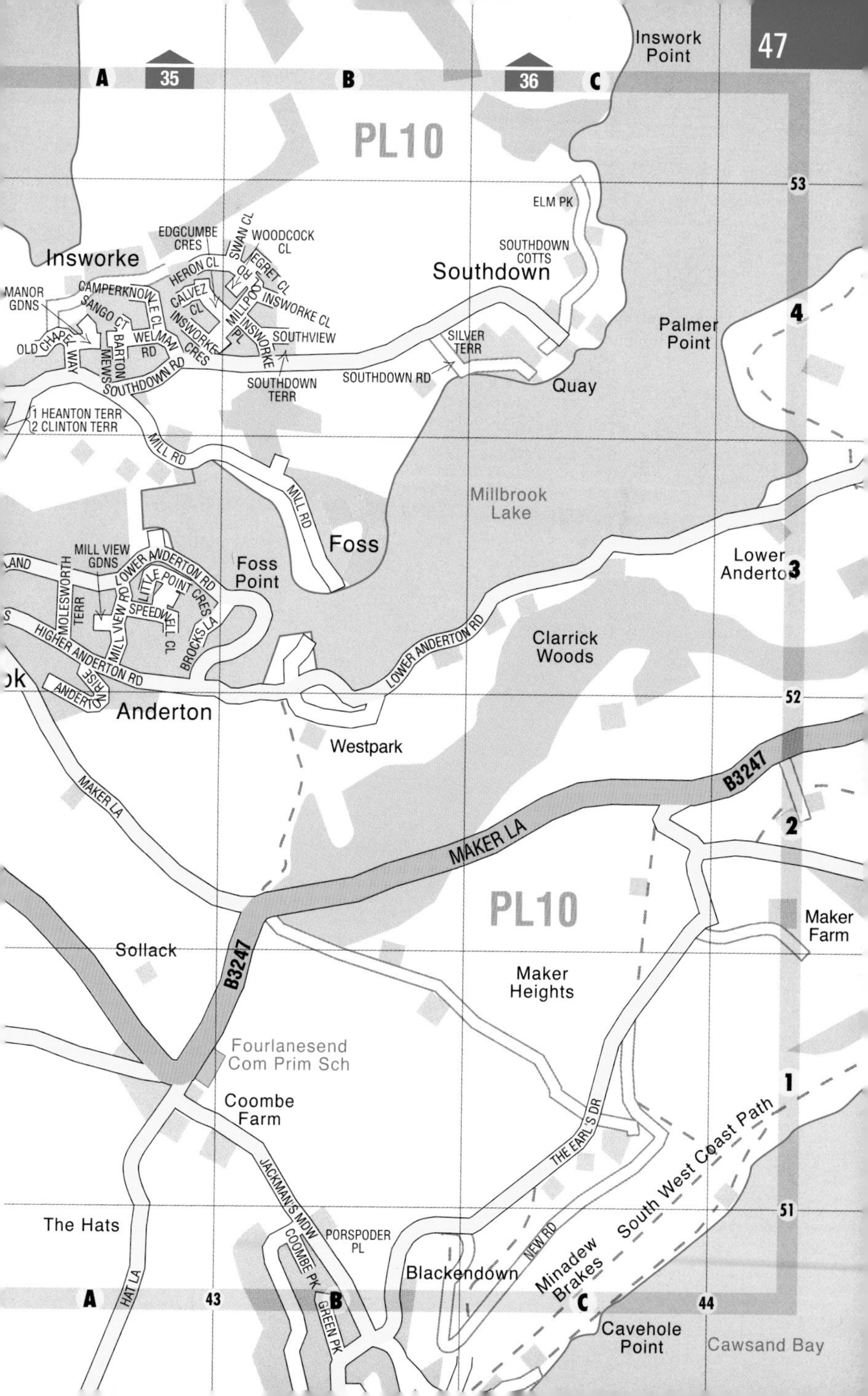
A
35
B
36
C
Inswork Point
PL10
53
ELM PK
EDGCUMBE CRES
SWAN CL
WOODCOCK CL
Insworke
SOUTHDOWN COTTS
Southdown
HERON CL
RD
EGRET CL
MANOR GDNS
CAMPERKNOWLE CL
CALVEZ CL
MILLPOOL
INSWORKE CL
4
SANGO CT
INSWORKE
Palmer Point
OLD CHAPEL WAY
BARTON MEWS
WELMAN RD
INSWORKE CRES
PL
SOUTHVIEW
SILVER TERR
SOUTHDOWN RD
SOUTHDOWN TERR
SOUTHDOWN RD
Quay
1 HEANTON TERR
2 CLINTON TERR
MILL RD
MILL RD
Millbrook Lake
Foss
MILL VIEW GDNS
LOWER ANDERTON RD
Foss Point
Lower Anderton
3
MOLESWORTH TERR
LITTLE POINT CRES
MILL VIEW RD
SPEEDWELL CL
BROCKS LA
HIGHER ANDERTON RD
LOWER ANDERTON RD
Clarrick Woods
ANDERTON RISE
Anderton
52
Westpark
MAKER LA
B3247
2
MAKER LA
PL10
Maker Farm
Sollack
B3247
Maker Heights
Fourlanesend Com Prim Sch
1
Coombe Farm
JACKMAN'S MDW
THE EARL'S DR
South West Coast Path
51
The Hats
PORSPODER PL
COOMBE PK
NEW RD
Blackendown
Minadew Brakes
A
43
B
C
44
HAT LA
GREEN PK
Cavehole Point
Cawsand Bay

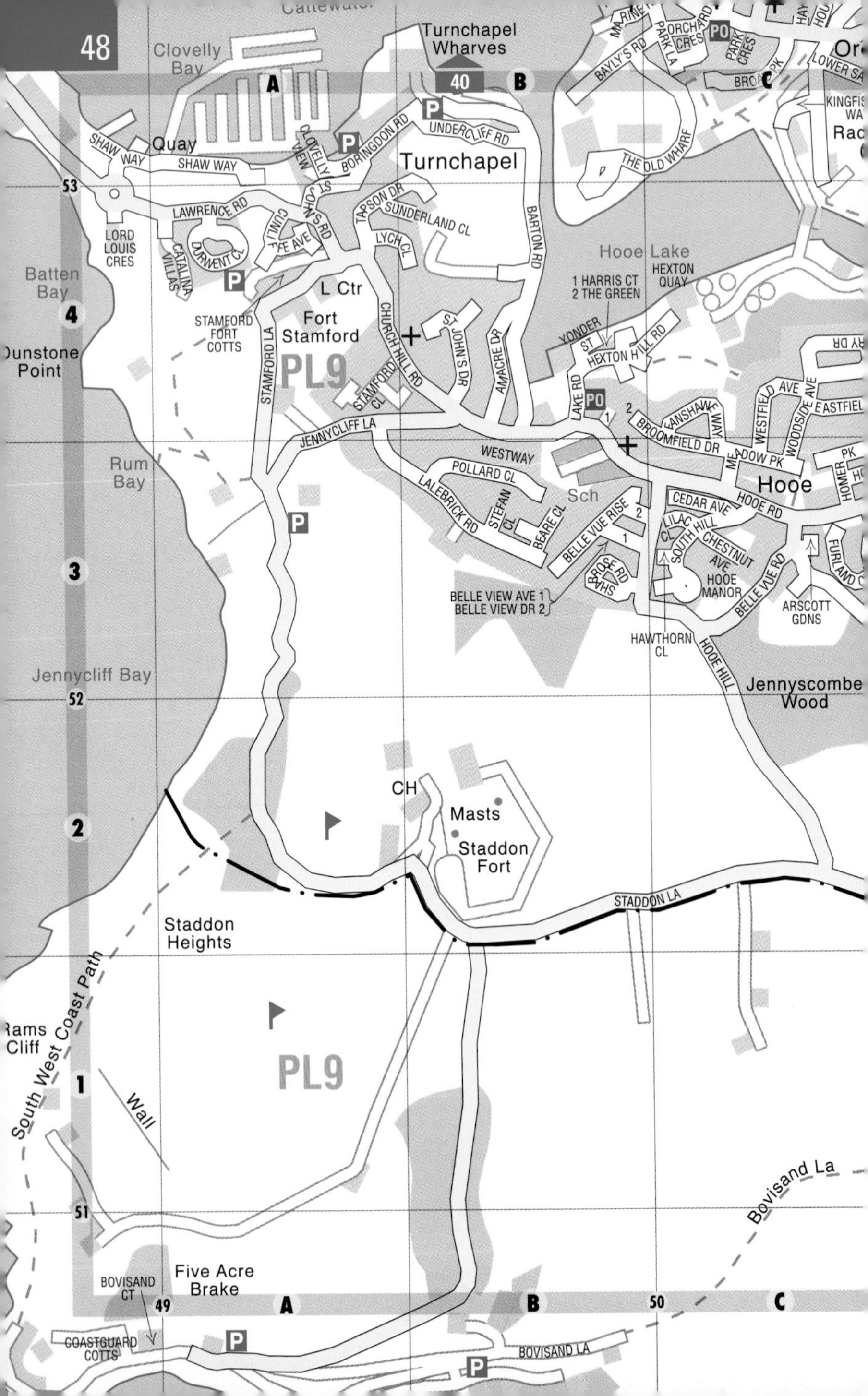
48
Clovelly Bay
Turnchapel Wharves
40
A
B
C
Quay
SHAW WAY
BORINGDON RD
UNDERCLIFF RD
CLOVELLY VIEW
ST JOHN'S RD
Turnchapel
LAWRENCE RD
TAPSON DR
SUNDERLAND CL
LORD LOUIS CRES
CATALINA VILLAS
DURWENT CL
FE AVE
LYCH CL
BARTON RD
Batten Bay
STAMFORD FORT COTTS
L Ctr
Fort Stamford
CHURCH HILL RD
ST JOHN'S DR
AMACRE DR
Dunstone Point
STAMFORD LA
PL9
STAMFORD CL
JENNYCLIFF LA
MARINE
PARK LA
ORCHARD CRES
PO
PARK CRES
BAYLY'S RD
BROAD PK
LOWER SA
KINGFIS WA
Rac
THE OLD WHARF
Hooe Lake
HEXTON QUAY
1 HARRIS CT
2 THE GREEN
YONDER ST
HEXTON HILL RD
LAKE RD
BROOMFIELD DR
HANSHAW WAY
WESTFIELD AVE
WOODSIDE AVE
EASTFIEL
MEADOW PK
WESTWAY
POLLARD CL
LALEBRICK RD
STEFAN CL
BEARE CL
Sch
BELLE VUE RISE
CEDAR AVE
HOOE RD
Hooe
HOMER PK
LILAC CL
SOUTH HILL
CHESTNUT AVE
HOOE MANOR
BELLE VUE RD
FURLAND CL
SHA BROSE RD
BELLE VIEW AVE 1
BELLE VIEW DR 2
ARSCOTT GDNS
HAWTHORN CL
HOOE HILL
Rum Bay
Jennycliff Bay
Jennyscombe Wood
53
4
3
52
2
1
51
49
50
CH
Masts
Staddon Fort
STADDON LA
Staddon Heights
South West Coast Path
Rams Cliff
Wall
Bovisand La
Five Acre Brake
BOVISAND CT
COASTGUARD COTTS
BOVISAND LA
P

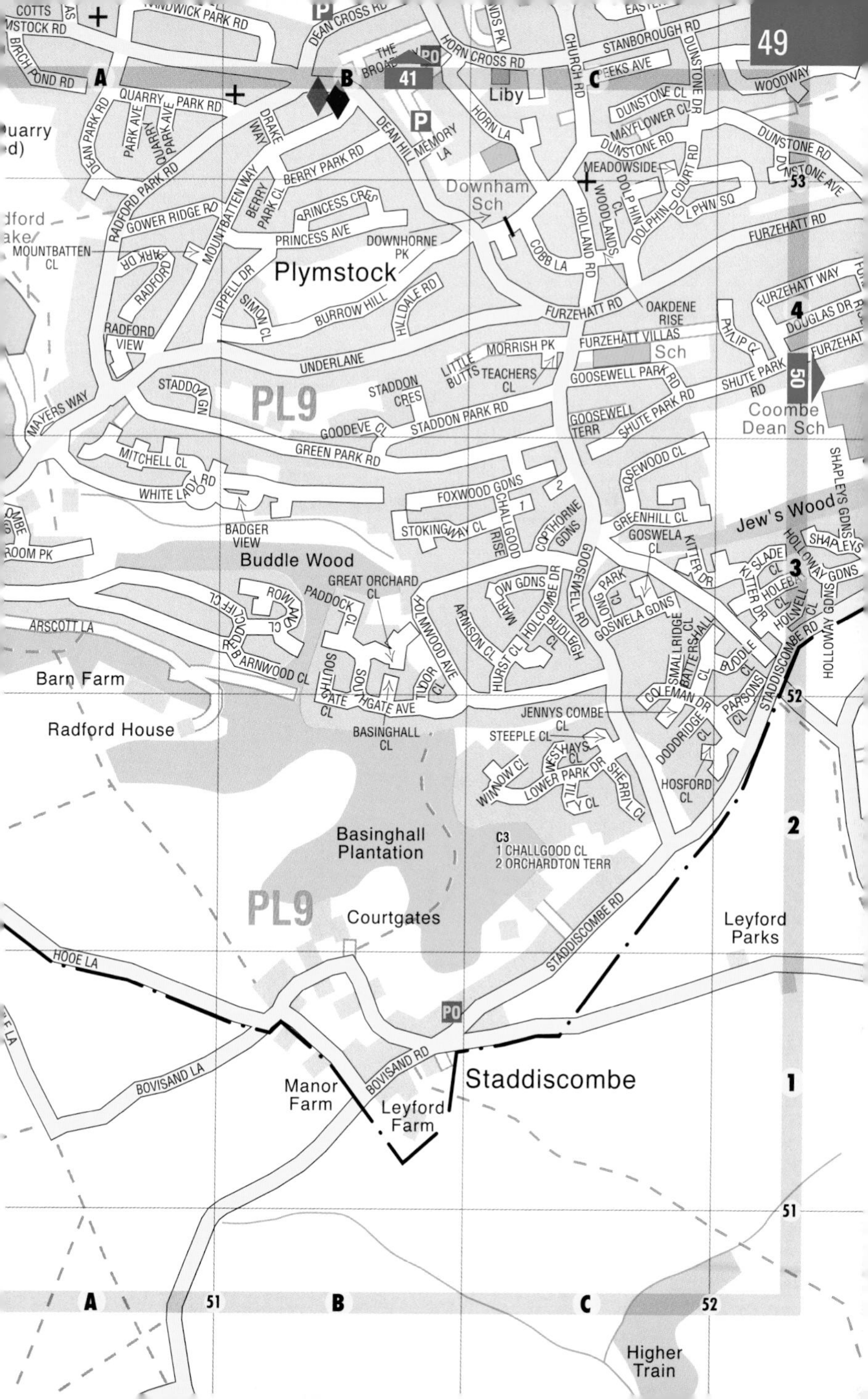

Plymstock
PL9
PL9
Staddiscombe
Buddle Wood
Basinghall Plantation
Courtgates
Barn Farm
Radford House
Manor Farm
Leyford Farm
Leyford Parks
Higher Train
Jew's Wood
Downham Sch
Sch
Coombe Dean Sch
Liby
PO
41
50
53
52
51
QUARRY PARK RD
PARK AVE
QUARRY PARK AVE
DEAN PARK RD
RADFORD PARK RD
DRAKE WAY
DEAN CROSS RD
THE BROADWAY
HORN CROSS RD
CHURCH RD
STANBOROUGH RD
DUNSTONE DR
WOODWAY
HORN LA
MEMORY LA
DEAN HILL
BERRY PARK RD
BERRY PARK CL
MOUNTBATTEN WAY
GOWER RIDGE RD
MOUNTBATTEN CL
PRINCESS CRES
PRINCESS AVE
DOWNHORNE PK
DUNSTONE CL
MAYFLOWER CL
DUNSTONE RD
DUNSTONE AVE
MEADOWSIDE
DOLPHIN CL
DOLPHIN SQ
DOLPHIN COURT RD
WOODLANDS
HOLLAND RD
COBB LA
FURZEHATT RD
FURZEHATT WAY
OAKDENE RISE
DOUGLAS DR
FURZEHATT VILLAS
PHILIP CL
RADFORD VIEW
LIPPELL DR
SIMON CL
BURROW HILL
HILLDALE RD
UNDERLANE
MORRISH PK
LITTLE BUTTS
TEACHERS CL
GOOSEWELL PARK RD
SHUTE PARK RD
STADDON GN
STADDON CRES
STADDON PARK RD
GOODEVE CL
GOOSEWELL TERR
MAYERS WAY
MITCHELL CL
GREEN PARK RD
WHITE LADY RD
BADGER VIEW
FOXWOOD GDNS
CHALLGOOD RISE
STOKINGWAY CL
COPTHORNE GDNS
ROSEWOOD CL
GREENHILL CL
GOSWELA CL
KITTER DR
SHAPLEYS GDNS
HOLLOWAY GDNS
SLADE CL
HOLEBAY CL
HOLWELL CL
GREAT ORCHARD CL
PADDOCK CL
ROWLAND CL
REDDICLIFF CL
ARSCOTT LA
ARNWOOD CL
HOLMWOOD AVE
MARLOW GDNS
HOLCOMBE DR
BUDLEIGH CL
ARMSON CL
HURST CL
GOOSEWELL RD
LONG PARK CL
GOSWELA GDNS
SMALLRIDGE CL
BATTERSHALL CL
BUDDLE CL
STADDISCOMBE RD
SOUTHGATE CL
SOUTHGATE AVE
TUDOR CL
BASINGHALL CL
JENNYS COMBE CL
STEEPLE CL
WESTHAYS CL
COLEMAN DR
PARSONS CL
DODDRIDGE CL
WINNOW CL
LOWER PARK DR
TILLY CL
SHERRILL CL
HOSFORD CL
C3
1 CHALLGOOD CL
2 ORCHARDTON TERR
HOOE LA
BOVISAND LA
BOVISAND RD
A
B
C
1
2
3
4

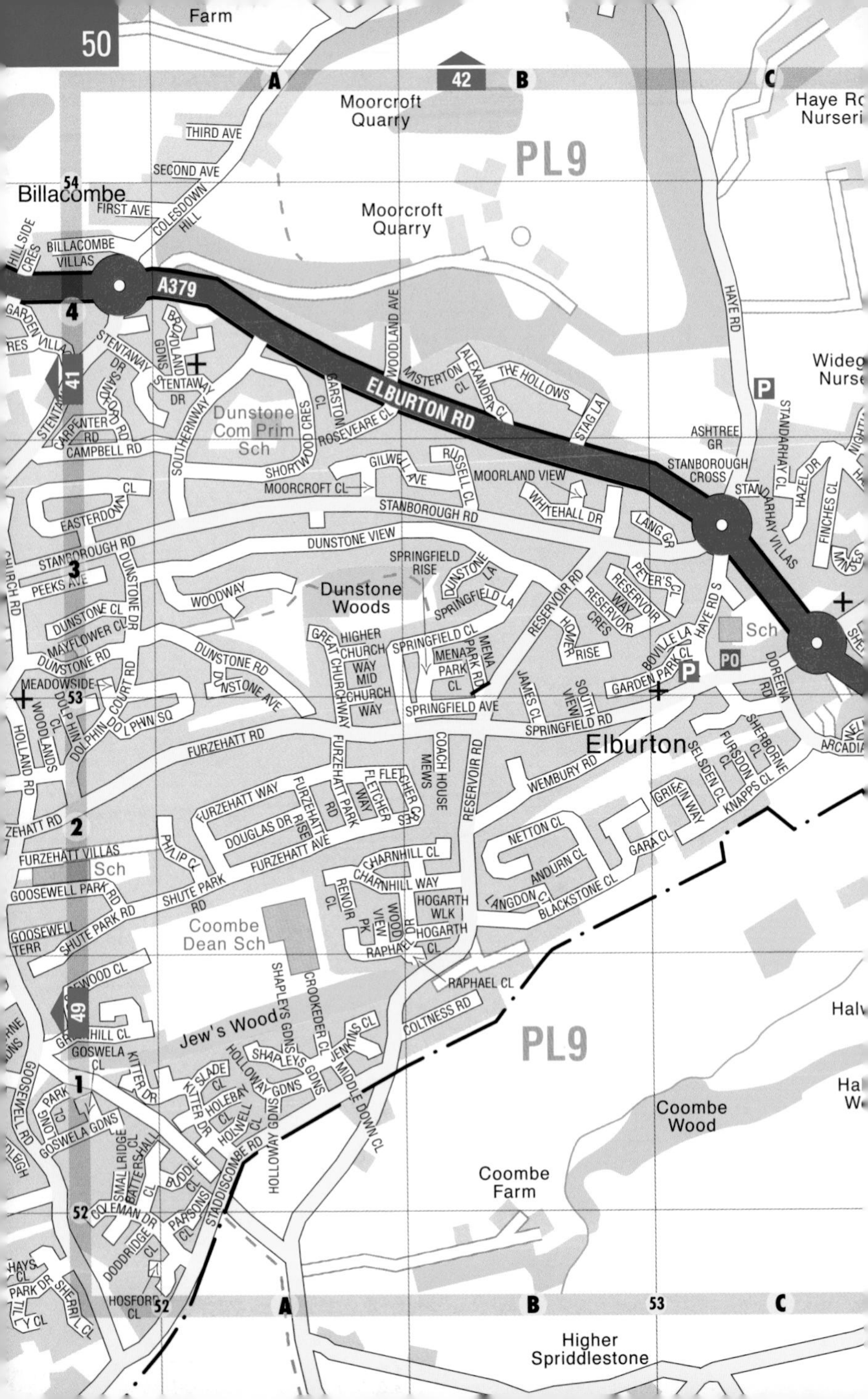

Farm
42
A
B
C
Moorcroft Quarry
Haye Rd Nurseries
PL9
Billacombe
THIRD AVE
SECOND AVE
FIRST AVE
COLESDOWN HILL
Moorcroft Quarry
HILLSIDE CRES
BILLACOMBE VILLAS
A379
ELBURTON RD
HAYE RD
Dunstone Com Prim Sch
Dunstone Woods
Elburton
Sch
Coombe Dean Sch
Jew's Wood
PL9
Coombe Wood
Coombe Farm
Higher Spriddlestone
STENTAWAY DR
BROADLAND GDNS
SOUTHERNWAY
CARPENTER RD
CAMPBELL RD
SHORTWOOD CRES
GARSTON CL
ROSEVEARE CL
WOODLAND AVE
MISTERTON CL
ALEXANDRA CL
THE HOLLOWS
STAG LA
ASHTREE GR
STANBOROUGH CROSS
STANDARHAY CL
STANDARHAY VILLAS
HAZEL DR
FINCHES CL
GILWELL AVE
RUSSELL CL
MOORLAND VIEW
MOORCROFT CL
WHITEHALL DR
STANBOROUGH RD
LANG GR
EASTERDOWN CL
DUNSTONE VIEW
SPRINGFIELD RISE
DUNSTONE LA
SPRINGFIELD LA
RESERVOIR RD
RESERVOIR WAY
RESERVOIR CRES
PETER'S CL
HAYE RD S
HOMER RISE
BOVILLE LA
GARDEN PARK CL
DOREENA RD
PEEKS AVE
WOODWAY
DUNSTONE DR
DUNSTONE CL
MAYFLOWER CL
DUNSTONE RD
GREAT CHURCHWAY
HIGHER CHURCH WAY
MID CHURCH WAY
SPRINGFIELD CL
MENA PARK CL
MENA PARK RD
SPRINGFIELD AVE
JAMES CL
SOUTH VIEW
SPRINGFIELD RD
MEADOWSIDE
DOLPHIN CL
DOLPHIN COURT RD
DOLPHIN SQ
DUNSTONE AVE
WOODLANDS
HOLLAND RD
FURZEHATT RD
FURZEHATT WAY
FURZEHATT PARK RD
FURZEHATT RISE
FLETCHER WAY
FLETCHER CRES
COACH HOUSE MEWS
WEMBURY RD
SELSDEN CL
FURSDON CL
SHERBORNE CL
KNAPPS CL
ARCADIA
GRIFFIN WAY
DOUGLAS DR
FURZEHATT AVE
NETTON CL
ANDURN CL
GARA CL
FURZEHATT VILLAS
PHILIP CL
CHARNHILL CL
CHARNHILL WAY
RENOIR CL
HOGARTH WLK
HOGARTH CL
LANGDON CL
BLACKSTONE CL
GOOSEWELL PARK RD
SHUTE PARK RD
GOOSEWELL TERR
VIEW PK
WOOD VIEW
RAPHAEL DR
RAPHAEL CL
SHAPLEYS GDNS
CROOKEDER CL
COLTNESS RD
GOSWELA CL
KITTER DR
SLADE CL
HOLEBAY CL
HOLWELL CL
HOLLOWAY GDNS
JENKINS CL
MIDDLE DOWN CL
LONG PARK CL
GOSWELA GDNS
GOOSEWELL RD
SMALLRIDGE CL
BATTERSHALL CL
BUDDLE CL
PARSONS CL
STADDISCOMBE RD
COLEMAN DR
DODDRIDGE CL
HAYS CL
PARK DR
SHERRIL CL
HOSFORD CL
52
53
54
1
2
3
4
41
49
A
B
C
Sch
PO
Halw

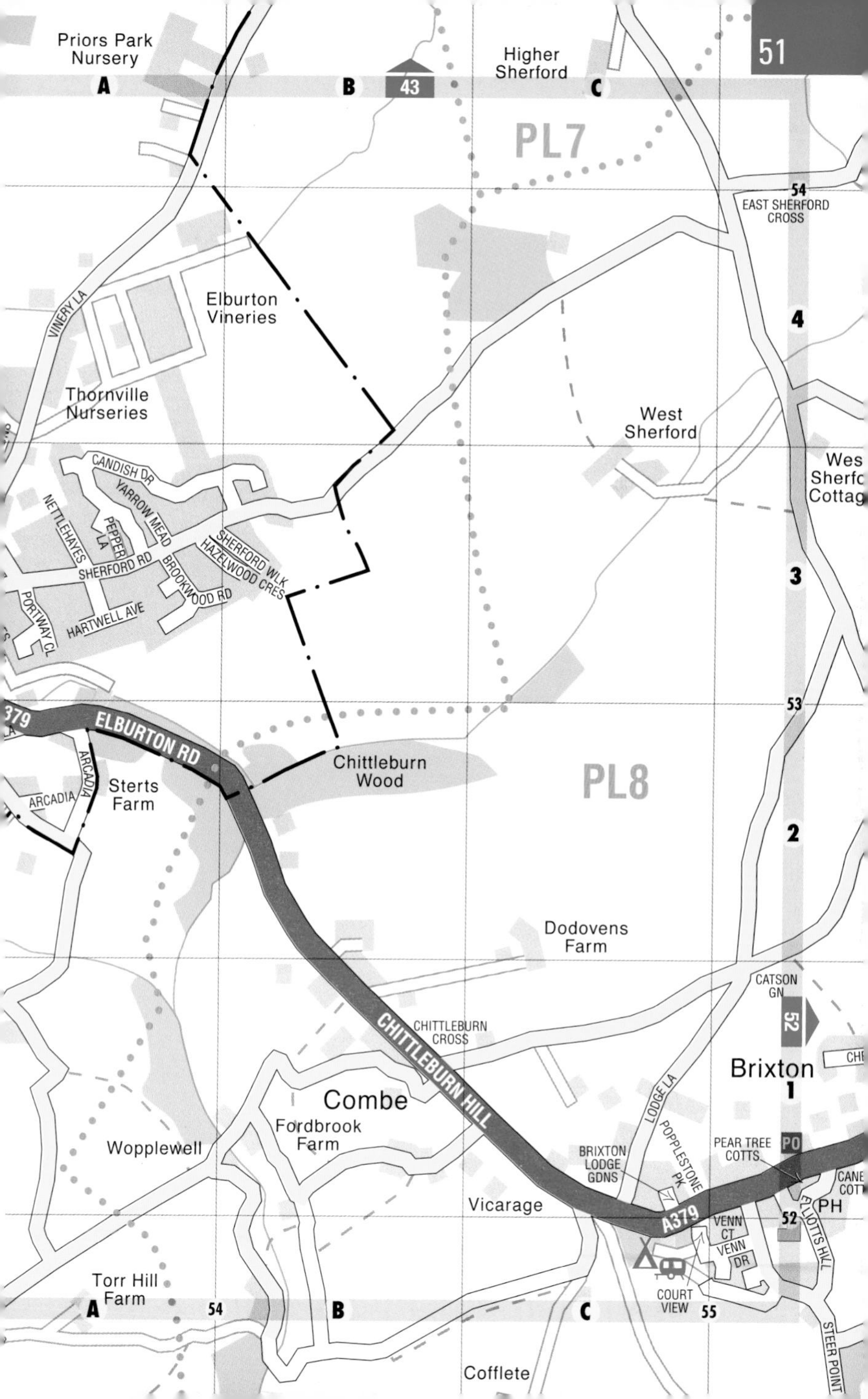

Priors Park Nursery
A
B
43
C
Higher Sherford
PL7
54
EAST SHERFORD CROSS
VINERY LA
Elburton Vineries
Thornville Nurseries
4
West Sherford
West Sherford Cottages
CANDISH DR
YARROW MEAD
NETTLEHAYES
PEPPER LA
SHERFORD RD
BROOKWOOD RD
SHERFORD WLK
HAZELWOOD CRES
PORTWAY CL
HARTWELL AVE
3
53
A379
ELBURTON RD
ARCADIA
Sterts Farm
Chittleburn Wood
PL8
2
Dodovens Farm
CATSON GN
52
CHITTLEBURN CROSS
CHITTLEBURN HILL
Combe
Brixton
1
LODGE LA
POPPLESTONE PK
Fordbrook Farm
Wopplewell
BRIXTON LODGE GDNS
PEAR TREE COTTS
PO
Vicarage
A379
VENN CT
VENN DR
ELLIOTTS HILL
PH
52
Torr Hill Farm
COURT VIEW
55
STEER POINT
Cofflete

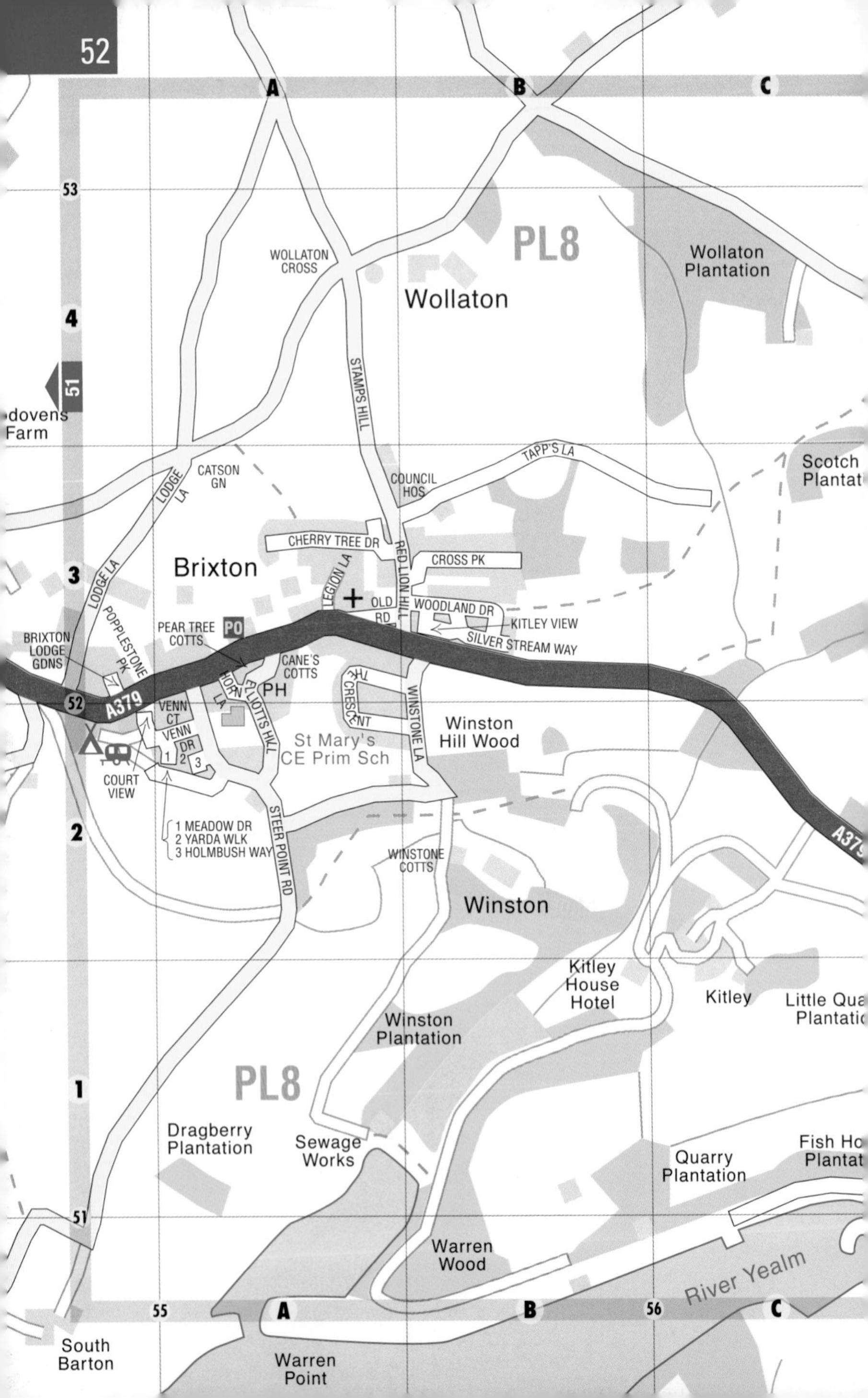
A
B
C
53
4
51
dovens
Farm
PL8
Wollaton
Plantation
WOLLATON
CROSS
Wollaton
STAMPS HILL
TAPP'S LA
Scotch
Plantat
COUNCIL
HOS
CATSON
GN
LODGE
LA
CHERRY TREE DR
RED LION HILL
CROSS PK
Brixton
3
LODGE LA
LEGION LA
OLD
RD
WOODLAND DR
KITLEY VIEW
SILVER STREAM WAY
POPPLESTONE
PK
PEAR TREE
COTTS
PO
BRIXTON
LODGE
GDNS
CANE'S
COTTS
THE
CRESCENT
HORN
LA
ELLIOTTS HILL
PH
52
A379
VENN
CT
VENN
DR
WINSTONE LA
Winston
Hill Wood
St Mary's
CE Prim Sch
COURT
VIEW
2
1 MEADOW DR
2 YARDA WLK
3 HOLMBUSH WAY
STEER POINT RD
WINSTONE
COTTS
Winston
A379
Kitley
House
Hotel
Kitley
Little Qua
Plantatic
Winston
Plantation
PL8
1
Dragberry
Plantation
Sewage
Works
Quarry
Plantation
Fish Ho
Plantat
51
Warren
Wood
River Yealm
55
A
B
56
C
South
Barton
Warren
Point

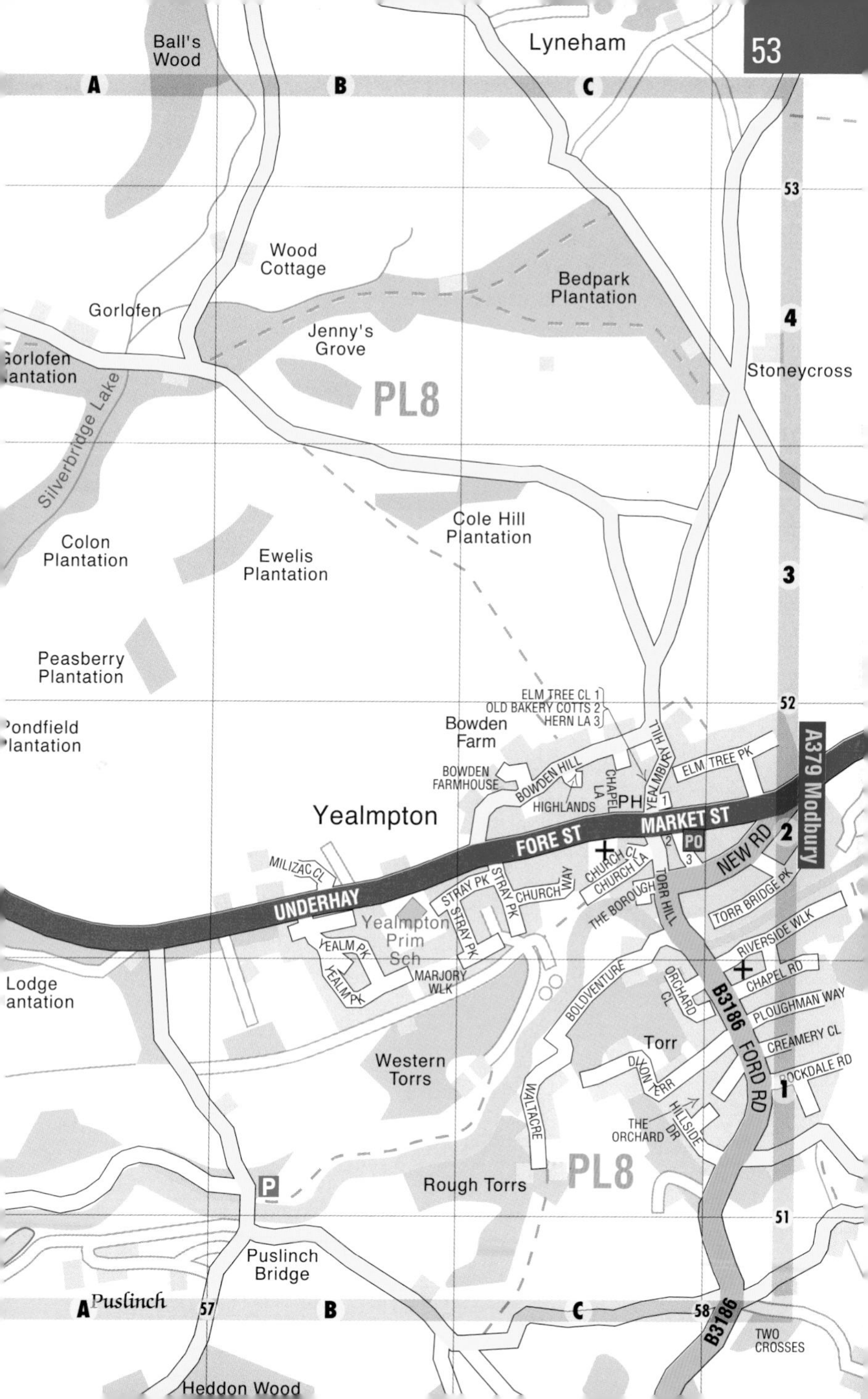

Ball's Wood
Lyneham
A
B
C
53
Wood Cottage
Bedpark Plantation
4
Gorlofen
Jenny's Grove
Gorlofen
lantation
Stoneycross
PL8
Silverbridge Lake
Cole Hill Plantation
Colon Plantation
Ewelis Plantation
3
Peasberry Plantation
ELM TREE CL 1
OLD BAKERY COTTS 2
HERN LA 3
52
Pondfield
lantation
Bowden Farm
A379 Modbury
BOWDEN FARMHOUSE
BOWDEN HILL
HIGHLANDS
CHAPEL LA
PH
YEALMBURY HILL
ELM TREE PK
Yealmpton
MARKET ST
FORE ST
PO
NEW RD
2
MILIZAC CL
CHURCH CL
CHURCH LA
CHURCH WAY
STRAY PK
TORR HILL
TORR BRIDGE PK
UNDERHAY
THE BOROUGH
Yealmpton Prim Sch
RIVERSIDE WLK
YEALM PK
MARJORY WLK
CHAPEL RD
Lodge
lantation
BOLDVENTURE
ORCHARD CL
B3186
PLOUGHMAN WAY
Torr
CREAMERY CL
Western Torrs
DIXON TERR
FORD RD
ROCKDALE RD
1
WALTACRE
THE ORCHARD
HILLSIDE DR
PL8
P
Rough Torrs
51
Puslinch Bridge
A
Puslinch
57
B
C
58
B3186
TWO CROSSES
Heddon Wood

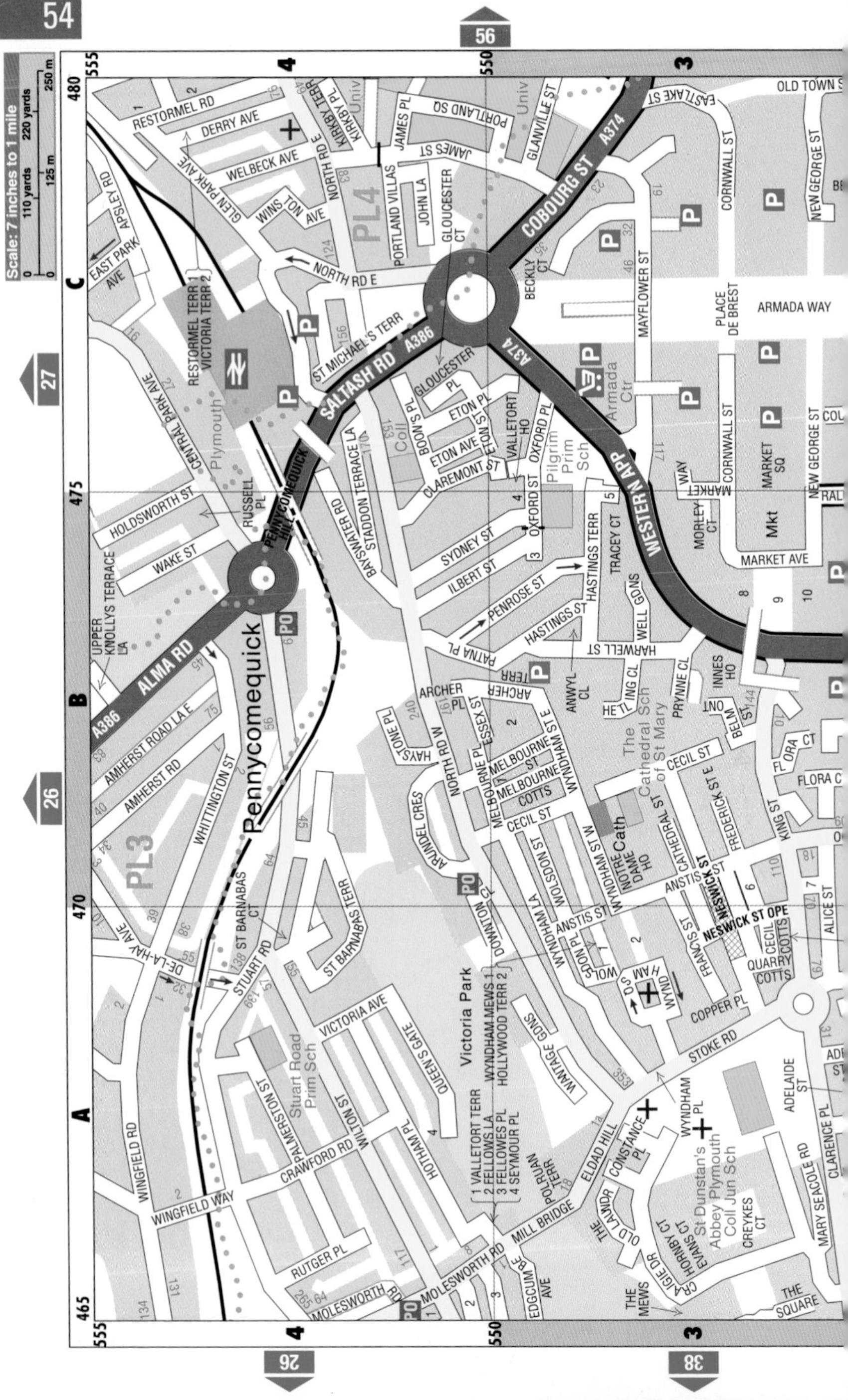

Scale: 7 inches to 1 mile
0 110 yards 220 yards
0 125 m 250 m

26
27
26
38
56

465 A 470 B 475 C 480
555 4 550 3

PL3
PL4
Pennycomequick
Victoria Park
Plymouth
Stuart Road Prim Sch
The Cathedral Sch of St Mary
Pilgrim Prim Sch
St Dunstan's Abbey Plymouth Coll Jun Sch
Armada Ctr
Coll
Univ
Cath
Mkt
PO
P

WINGFIELD RD
WINGFIELD WAY
DE-LA-HAY AVE
WHITTINGTON ST
AMHERST RD
AMHERST ROAD LA E
ALMA RD
A386
UPPER KNOLLYS TERRACE LA
WAKE ST
HOLDSWORTH ST
CENTRAL PARK AVE
RUSSELL PL
EAST PARK AVE
APSLEY RD
RESTORMEL TERR 1
VICTORIA TERR 2
RESTORMEL RD
DERRY AVE
GLEN PARK AVE
WELBECK AVE
WINSTON AVE
NORTH RD E
KIRKBY TERR
KIRKBY PL
STUART RD
ST BARNABAS CT
ST BARNABAS TERR
PALMERSTON ST
CRAWFORD RD
WILTON ST
VICTORIA AVE
RUTGER PL
MOLESWORTH RD
HOTHAM PL
QUEEN'S GATE
PENNYCOMEQUICK HILL
SALTASH RD
ST MICHAEL'S TERR
BAYSWATER RD
STADDON TERRACE LA
PORTLAND VILLAS
JAMES PL
JOHN LA
JAMES ST
PORTLAND SQ
GLOUCESTER CT
GLOUCESTER PL
BOON'S PL
ETON AVE
ETON ST
ETON PL
CLAREMONT ST
HAYSTONE PL
ARUNDEL CRES
NORTH RD W
ARCHER PL
ARCHER TERR
PATNA PL
ILBERT ST
SYDNEY ST
PENROSE ST
OXFORD ST
OXFORD PL
VALLETORT HO
A374
COBOURG ST
BECKLY CT
GLANVILLE ST
1 VALLETORT TERR
2 FELLOWS LA
3 FELLOWES PL
4 SEYMOUR PL
WYNDHAM MEWS 1
HOLLYWOOD TERR 2
DOWNTON CL
MELBOURNE PL
ESSEX ST
MELBOURNE COTTS
MELBOURNE ST
WYNDHAM ST E
CECIL ST
WYNDHAM LA
WOLSDON ST
WOLSDON PL
ANSTIS ST
WYNDHAM ST W
NOTRE DAME HO
EDGCUMBE AVE
MILL BRIDGE
POLRUAN TERR
WANTAGE GDNS
ELDAD HILL
THE OLD LAUNDRY
CONSTANCE PL
THE MEWS
CRAIGIE DR
HORNBY CT
EVANS CT
CREYKES CT
WYNDHAM PL
WYNDHAM SQ
STOKE RD
COPPER PL
FRANCIS ST
CATHEDRAL ST
NESWICK ST
NESWICK ST OPE
FREDERICK ST E
QUARRY COTTS
CECIL COTTS
KING ST
FLORA CT
FLORA CL
ALICE ST
ADELAIDE ST
MARY SEACOLE RD
CLARENCE PL
THE SQUARE
ANWYL CL
HASTINGS ST
HASTINGS TERR
HARWELL ST
HETLING CL
WELL GDNS
TRACEY CT
PRYNNE CL
BELMONT ST
INNES HO
WESTERN APP
MAYFLOWER ST
MORLEY CT
MARKET WAY
MARKET AVE
MARKET SQ
CORNWALL ST
PLACE DE BREST
ARMADA WAY
NEW GEORGE ST
EASTLAKE ST
OLD TOWN ST

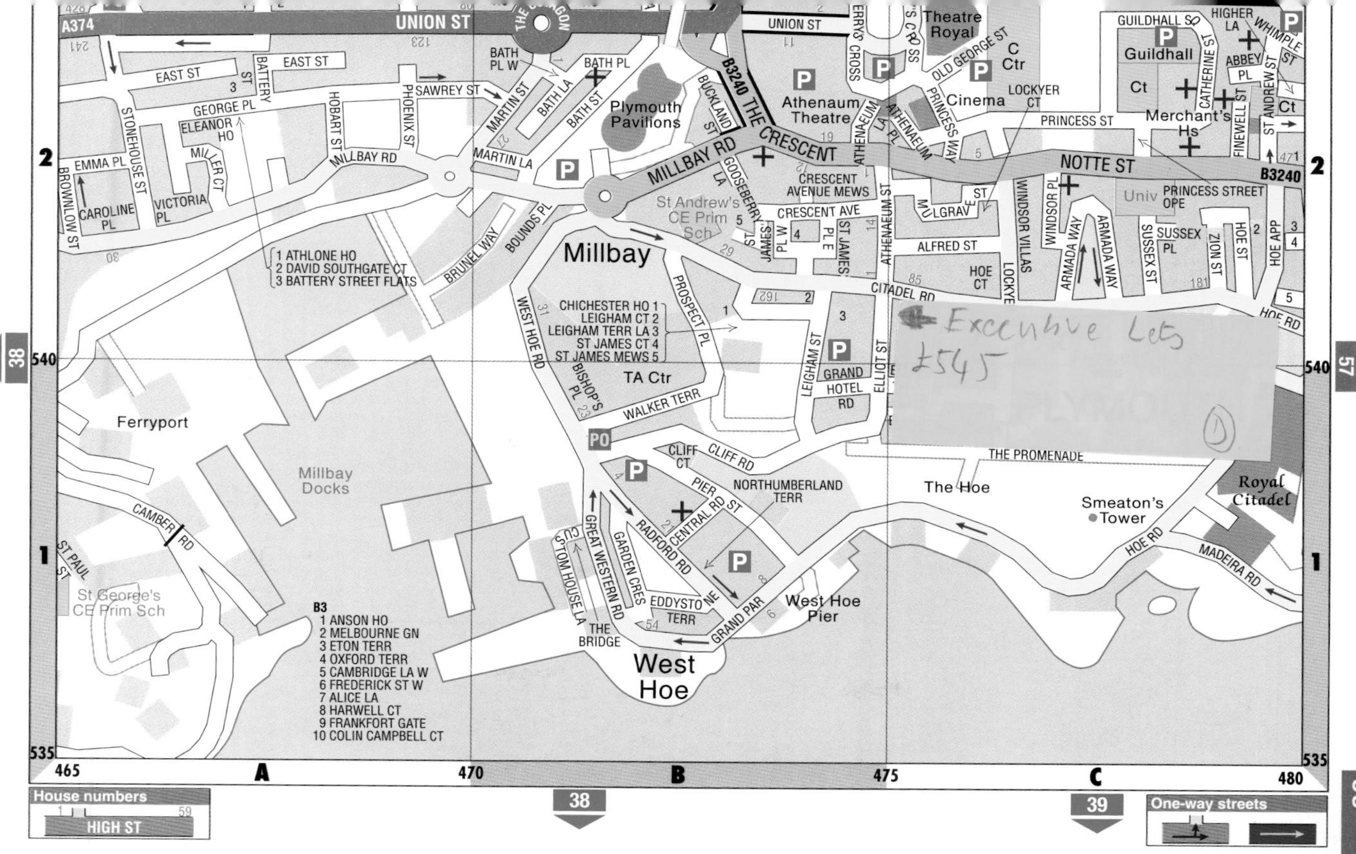
A374
UNION ST
THE OCTAGON
EAST ST
BATTERY ST
BATH PL W
BATH PL
BATH LA
BATH ST
MARTIN ST
SAWREY ST
PHOENIX ST
HOBART ST
GEORGE PL
ELEANOR HO
MILLER CT
STONEHOUSE ST
EMMA PL
CAROLINE PL
VICTORIA PL
BROWNLOW ST
MILLBAY RD
MARTIN LA
Plymouth Pavilions
BUCKLAND ST
B3240 THE CRESCENT
Athenaum Theatre
DERRY'S CROSS
Theatre Royal
OLD GEORGE ST
C Ctr
Cinema
LOCKYER CT
PRINCESS WAY
ATHENAEUM LA
ATHENAEUM PL
PRINCESS ST
NOTTE ST
B3240
GUILDHALL SQ
Guildhall
Ct
CATHERINE ST
Merchant's Hs
HIGHER LA
WHIMPLE ST
ABBEY PL
ST ANDREW ST
FINEWELL ST
St Andrew's CE Prim Sch
GOOSEBERRY LA
CRESCENT AVENUE MEWS
CRESCENT AVE
ST JAMES PL W
ST JAMES PL E
ATHENAEUM ST
MULGRAVE ST
WINDSOR VILLAS
WINDSOR PL
ARMADA WAY
Univ
PRINCESS STREET OPE
SUSSEX ST
SUSSEX PL
ZION ST
HOE ST
HOE APP
ALFRED ST
HOE CT
LOCKYER
CITADEL RD
HOE RD
BOUNDS PL
BRUNEL WAY
1 ATHLONE HO
2 DAVID SOUTHGATE CT
3 BATTERY STREET FLATS
Millbay
WEST HOE RD
PROSPECT PL
CHICHESTER HO 1
LEIGHAM CT 2
LEIGHAM TERR LA 3
ST JAMES CT 4
ST JAMES MEWS 5
TA Ctr
BISHOP'S PL
WALKER TERR
LEIGHAM ST
GRAND HOTEL RD
ELLIOT ST
PO
CLIFF CT
CLIFF RD
PIER ST
NORTHUMBERLAND TERR
CENTRAL RD
RADFORD RD
GARDEN CRES
GREAT WESTERN RD
CUSTOM HOUSE LA
EDDYSTONE TERR
GRAND PAR
THE BRIDGE
West Hoe
West Hoe Pier
THE PROMENADE
The Hoe
Smeaton's Tower
Royal Citadel
MADEIRA RD
Ferryport
Millbay Docks
CAMBER RD
ST PAUL ST
St George's CE Prim Sch
B3
1 ANSON HO
2 MELBOURNE GN
3 ETON TERR
4 OXFORD TERR
5 CAMBRIDGE LA W
6 FREDERICK ST W
7 ALICE LA
8 HARWELL CT
9 FRANKFORT GATE
10 COLIN CAMPBELL CT
540
535
465
A
470
B
475
C
480
1
2
38
57
38
39
House numbers
HIGH ST
One-way streets

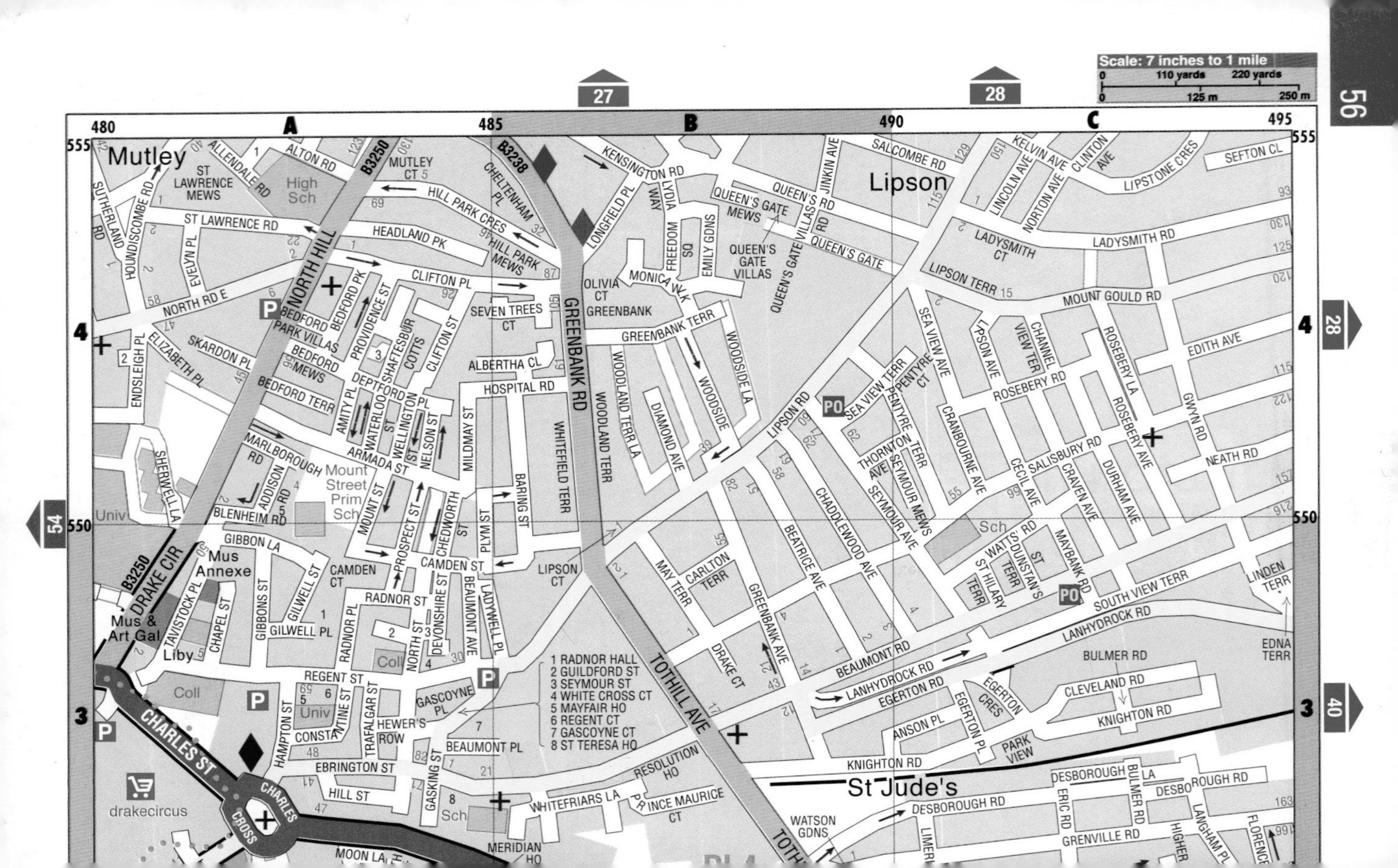

Scale: 7 inches to 1 mile
0 110 yards 220 yards
0 125 m 250 m
27
28
40
54
A
B
C
3
4
Mutley
Lipson
St Jude's
GREENBANK RD
TOTHILL AVE
NORTH HILL
DRAKE CIR
CHARLES ST
CHARLES CROSS
B3238
B3250
LIPSON RD
MOUNT GOULD RD
LADYSMITH RD
LANHYDROCK RD
BEAUMONT RD
KNIGHTON RD
DESBOROUGH RD
GREENBANK AVE
BEATRICE AVE
CHADDLEWOOD AVE
SEYMOUR AVE
ROSEBERY AVE
GWYN RD
EDITH AVE
NEATH RD
SALISBURY RD
CECIL AVE
CRANBOURNE AVE
SEA VIEW AVE
LIPSON TERR
QUEEN'S GATE
WOODSIDE
WOODLAND TERR
WHITEFIELD TERR
BARING ST
MILDMAY ST
CLIFTON PL
HILL PARK CRES
HEADLAND PK
MUTLEY CT
ALTON RD
ST LAWRENCE RD
NORTH RD E
HOUNDISCOMBE RD
SUTHERLAND RD
BEDFORD PK
ARMADA ST
MOUNT ST
CAMDEN ST
GASKING ST
EBRINGTON ST
HILL ST
MOON LA
1 RADNOR HALL
2 GUILDFORD ST
3 SEYMOUR ST
4 WHITE CROSS CT
5 MAYFAIR HO
6 REGENT CT
7 GASCOYNE CT
8 ST TERESA HO
drakecircus

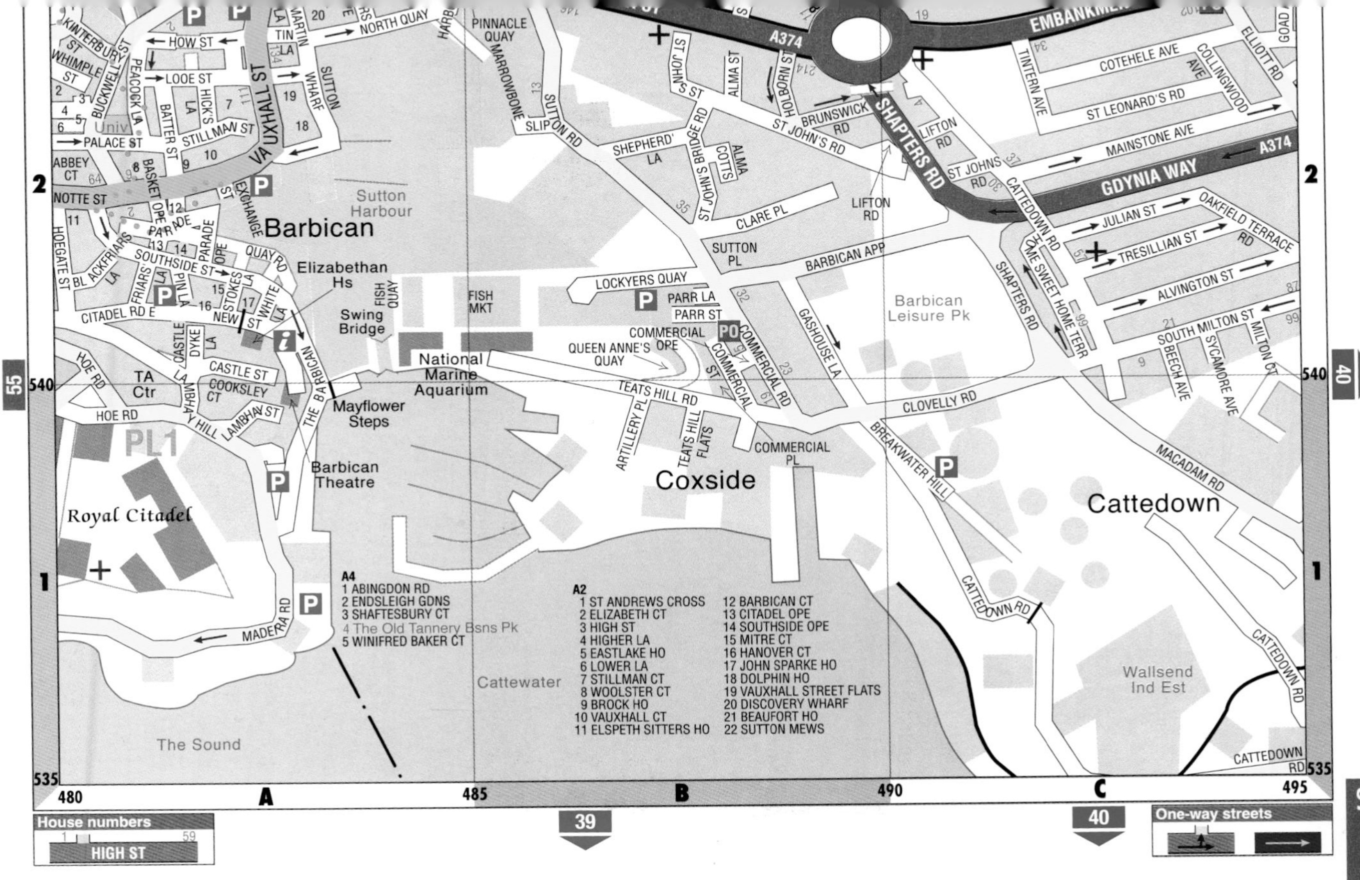
Barbican
Sutton Harbour
Coxside
Cattedown
Barbican Leisure Pk
Wallsend Ind Est
Cattewater
The Sound
Royal Citadel
PL1
National Marine Aquarium
Mayflower Steps
Barbican Theatre
Elizabethan Hs
Swing Bridge
FISH MKT
FISH QUAY
TA Ctr
Univ
EMBANKMENT
A374
GDYNIA WAY
SHAPTERS RD
VAUXHALL ST
NORTH QUAY
SUTTON WHARF
PINNACLE QUAY
MARROWBONE SLIP
SUTTON RD
HOW ST
LOOE ST
PEACOCK LA
BATTER ST
HICK'S LA
STILLMAN ST
PALACE ST
ABBEY CT
NOTTE ST
HOEGATE ST
BLACKFRIARS LA
FRIARS' LA
SOUTHSIDE ST
PARADE
BASKET OPE
EXCHANGE ST
QUAY RD
STOKES LA
WHITE LA
NEW ST
PIN LA
CITADEL RD E
CASTLE DYKE LA
CASTLE ST
COOKSLEY CT
LAMBHAY HILL
LAMBHAY ST
HOE RD
MADEIRA RD
THE BARBICAN
KINTERBURY ST
WHIMPLE ST
BUCKWELL ST
MARTIN
TIN LA
ST JOHN'S ST
ALMA ST
HOLBORN ST
BRUNSWICK RD
ST JOHN'S RD
SHEPHERD' LA
ST JOHN'S BRIDGE RD
ALMA COTTS
CLARE PL
SUTTON PL
BARBICAN APP
LIFTON RD
ST JOHNS RD
LOCKYERS QUAY
PARR LA
PARR ST
COMMERCIAL OPE
QUEEN ANNE'S QUAY
COMMERCIAL ST
COMMERCIAL RD
GASHOUSE LA
TEATS HILL RD
ARTILLERY PL
TEATS HILL FLATS
COMMERCIAL PL
CLOVELLY RD
BREAKWATER HILL
CATTEDOWN RD
SHAPTERS RD
HOME SWEET HOME TERR
MACADAM RD
TINTERN AVE
COTEHELE AVE
COLLINGWOOD AVE
ST LEONARD'S RD
ELLIOTT RD
GOAD
MAINSTONE AVE
JULIAN ST
TRESILLIAN ST
OAKFIELD TERRACE RD
ALVINGTON ST
SOUTH MILTON ST
MILTON CT
BEECH AVE
SYCAMORE AVE
A4
1 ABINGDON RD
2 ENDSLEIGH GDNS
3 SHAFTESBURY CT
4 The Old Tannery Bsns Pk
5 WINIFRED BAKER CT
A2
1 ST ANDREWS CROSS
2 ELIZABETH CT
3 HIGH ST
4 HIGHER LA
5 EASTLAKE HO
6 LOWER LA
7 STILLMAN CT
8 WOOLSTER CT
9 BROCK HO
10 VAUXHALL CT
11 ELSPETH SITTERS HO
12 BARBICAN CT
13 CITADEL OPE
14 SOUTHSIDE OPE
15 MITRE CT
16 HANOVER CT
17 JOHN SPARKE HO
18 DOLPHIN HO
19 VAUXHALL STREET FLATS
20 DISCOVERY WHARF
21 BEAUFORT HO
22 SUTTON MEWS
480
A
485
B
490
C
495
535
540
1
2
55
40
39
House numbers
HIGH ST
One-way streets

Index

Street names are listed alphabetically and show the locality, the Postcode district, the page number and a reference to the square in which the name falls on the map page

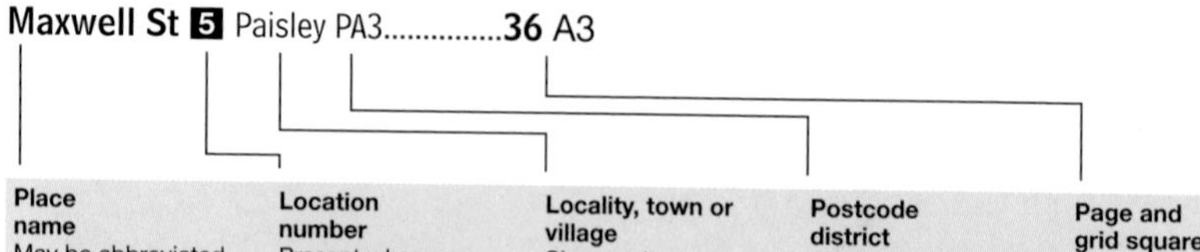

Place name
May be abbreviated on the map

Location number
Present when a number indicates the place's position in a crowded area of mapping

Locality, town or village
Shown when more than one place has the same name

Postcode district
District for the indexed place

Page and grid square
Page number and grid reference for the standard mapping

Towns and villages are listed in CAPITAL LETTERS

Public and commercial buildings are highlighted in magenta. **Places of interest** are highlighted in blue with a star

Abbreviations used in the index

Acad	Academy	Ct	Court	Hts	Heights	Pl	Place
App	Approach	Ctr	Centre	Ind	Industrial	Prec	Precinct
Arc	Arcade	Ctry	Country	Inst	Institute	Prom	Promenade
Ave	Avenue	Cty	County	Int	International	Rd	Road
Bglw	Bungalow	Dr	Drive	Intc	Interchange	Recn	Recreation
Bldg	Building	Dro	Drove	Junc	Junction	Ret	Retail
Bsns, Bus	Business	Ed	Education	L	Leisure	Sh	Shopping
Bvd	Boulevard	Emb	Embankment	La	Lane	Sq	Square
Cath	Cathedral	Est	Estate	Liby	Library	St	Street
Cir	Circus	Ex	Exhibition	Mdw	Meadow	Sta	Station
Cl	Close	Gd	Ground	Meml	Memorial	Terr	Terrace
Cnr	Corner	Gdn	Garden	Mkt	Market	TH	Town Hall
Coll	College	Gn	Green	Mus	Museum	Univ	University
Com	Community	Gr	Grove	Orch	Orchard	Wk, Wlk	Walk
Comm	Common	H	Hall	Pal	Palace	Wr	Water
Cott	Cottage	Ho	House	Par	Parade	Yd	Yard
Cres	Crescent	Hospl	Hospital	Pas	Passage		
Cswy	Causeway	HQ	Headquarters	Pk	Park		

Index of towns, villages, streets, hospitals, industrial estates, railway stations, schools, shopping centres, universities and places of interest

Abb–Ans

A

B

H

M

N

O

P

S

Y

Z

List of numbered locations

In some busy areas of the maps it is not always possible to show the name of every place.

Where not all names will fit, some smaller places are shown by a number. If you wish to find out the name associated with a number, use this listing.

The places in this list are also listed normally in the Index.

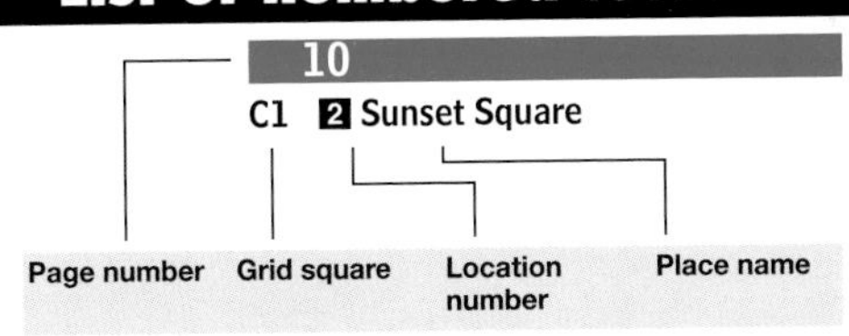